Contents

List of figures and table

SPENDING ON HEALTH CARE

How much is enough?

John Appleby and Anthony Harrison

Investment in the NHS has increased significantly under the Blair government. Spending will soon reach the EU average, but when we catch up with our European neighbours, what then? Assuming that pressures to spend more will continue, but that marginal health returns on extra investment are likely to diminish, this paper asks the question: when will enough be enough? In particular, can a limit on health spending be defined, and if so, how? And what evidence is required to inform what is ultimately a political decision?

Published in the United Kingdom by the King's Fund

© King's Fund 2006

Charity registration number: 207401

First published 2006

Reprinted 2006

A catalogue record for this publication is available from the British Library.

ISBN-10: 1 85717 543 3
ISBN-13: 978 1 85717 543 1

Available from:
King's Fund
11–13 Cavendish Square
London W1G 0AN
Tel: 020 7307 2591
Fax: 020 7307 2801
Email: publications@kingsfund.org.uk
www.kingsfund.org.uk/publications

Edited by First Draft Consultancy Ltd
Typeset by Andrew Haig and Associates
Printed and bound in Great Britain by Hobbs

About the authors

John Appleby is Chief Economist in Health Policy at the King's Fund. John has researched and published widely on many aspects of health service funding, rationing, resource allocation and performance. He previously worked as an economist with the NHS in Birmingham and London, and at the universities of Birmingham and East Anglia as Senior Lecturer in health economics. He is a visiting professor at the Department of Economics at City University. John has recently completed an independent review of health and social care provision in Northern Ireland.

Anthony Harrison is a Fellow in Health Policy at the King's Fund. Tony has published extensively on the future of hospital care in the United Kingdom, the private finance initiative and waiting list management, and has recently published a study of publicly funded research and development.

Acknowledgements

We would like to thank Seán Boyle, Professor Howard Glennerster, Jennifer Dixon and Niall Dickson for helpful comments on earlier drafts of this paper.

Summary

Throughout the United Kingdom, but most particularly in England, the Blair government has injected large increases of funding into the NHS with the intention of bringing health spending up to the European average. The (English) NHS is now six years into a nine year period of committed extra spending where annual real terms spending growth has so far averaged around seven per cent.

The government's decision to significantly increase investment reflects the political importance it attaches to health. However, with rising public expectations about the quality of health care and the inexorable growth in new (and generally more costly) ways of improving health-related quality and length of life through medical technology, pressures on spending are only likely to increase.

If health spending does not reach a plateau in the near future – as suggested by Derek Wanless's 2000 review – by 2026 the United Kingdom could be spending one pound of every five in the economy on health care. And, stretching such projections to their limit, in 40 years' time, if growth in health care spending continues to outstrip growth in the economy, half of the nation's wealth would be spent on health care.

But at the relatively high current levels of spending, the rate of increase in health benefits of spending (even) more on health care are likely to become increasingly slight. Therefore the case for higher public spending on health will become harder to make in terms of the returns on this investment.

This paper therefore asks the question: when will 'enough be enough'? Can a limit on health spending be defined? If so, how? And what evidence is required to inform what is ultimately a political decision?

The economics of health spending

In economic terms, spending on health, as on any other good, is worthwhile as long as the benefits it brings exceed those which could be obtained by other forms of spending. The usual assumption is that as spending in a particular area rises there inevitably comes a point where the additional benefits gained start to fall. It might also be possible for the absolute benefits to fall as spending increases still further. There is no reason why this pattern should be any different for health spending.

But the returns (that is, the health benefits) on investment in health care are not static and can change over time because:

- the cost of provision may rise or fall so that at every level of spending more (or less) benefits are produced
- the nature and extent of ill health in the population may rise, increasing the need for treatment and the potential benefits from spending more

- the 'value' attached to health benefits may change for a variety of reasons
- new treatments may be introduced due to technological changes – while some may reduce the cost of treatment, others are likely to cost more.

From the perspective of an economic evaluation, increased spending on health care is not inherently bad or undesirable. The full calculation requires information about the 'opportunity costs' of the inputs to health care as well as the value of the benefits of the outputs.

However, clear-cut conclusions are difficult to reach because of statistical limitations in two areas. First, it is hard to make specific links between any one intervention and recorded changes in health care. Second, there are problems with establishing how to measure the overall health benefits of health spending, taking into account improvements in factors like quality of life.

It is therefore virtually impossible for any one study to undertake a comprehensive and unambiguous assessment of the total returns to health care investment, including all sources of benefits and negative consequences. Nevertheless, there is scope for considerable improvement in monitoring and evaluating health spending so as to help better inform future decision making.

The development of evidence-based practice and the establishment of institutions such as National Institute for Health and Clinical Excellence (NICE) are attempts to begin to evaluate and regulate potential new health care costs. But such institutional innovations only address some of the problems. Influencing how users and health professionals actually behave, rather than the merits or disadvantages of particular technologies judged in trial conditions, require different measures (see 'Can a limit be set to spending?').

What is extra spending on the NHS producing now?

This lack of definitive data in many key areas means that it is impossible to come to a firm conclusion as to whether the NHS is generating positive, declining or negative returns on the current additional investment in health.

Gains are being achieved in areas such as convenience and process benefits, for example, the changes that have led to shorter waiting times within hospital accident and emergency departments. Some of these may lead to better health outcomes, but the main argument used by the government for setting targets such as these derives from the perception that 'expectations' of service performance are rising and that people want choice of when and where to be treated, and easier access to whatever services they choose. While this is convincing intuitively, there is in fact very little hard evidence about the value placed on benefits of these kinds, nor indeed of the costs of providing them.

The government is implementing a series of service reforms in the NHS aimed at improving the design and delivery of care, health outcomes and user experience. But there is currently no framework that attempts to identify the health benefits that are likely to be forthcoming from any of these initiatives. What is needed to address this is a benefits–cost matrix, similar to a programme budgeting approach (the full paper sets out an example of how such a matrix might be developed). The central problem of such an approach – as in programme budgeting – is attaching a value to the benefits and costs associated with different types of outcomes and different spending/policy areas.

The government could have used a matrix of this kind to present an explicit justification or business case for the extra resources it has decided to allocate to the NHS from 2000 onwards. It would also have served as a benchmark against which progress and achievement could have been measured in the years which have followed.

Can a limit be set for spending on health?

Controlling health care spending is a problem that all industrialised countries face and one which the United Kingdom will, after a long period of relative underfunding, also have to grapple with. This is underlined by the experiences of higher spending countries which clearly have still not reached a point where it has been possible to say that current levels of funding are 'enough'.

Any decision on setting a limit or threshold for funding should rely on an informed view of the likely benefits that further spending on health care will achieve. However, the information on which to base any judgement on the health returns resulting from the current significant increases in the NHS budget is poor. Evidence from countries that spend more than the United Kingdom suggests the health gains from the higher spending levels projected for the coming three to four years may not be large. But the narrow range of outcome measures available means that only limited weight can be put on such data.

Pressures to spend more will continue, so the aim is not to define an end point but rather a *means*, when budgets have to be set, of determining whether the returns from more spending are greater than their opportunity costs. This would need to be responsive to changing technology, shifts in what society values and so on.

Ultimately any threshold on health spending will be a political judgment: a limit is already set as part of a political process culminating in announcements by the Chancellor in budgets and spending reviews.

However, this political process needs to be informed by appropriate evidence. While the current assessment work of NICE goes some way to addressing the technical issues involved in producing the information on which a judgement about limits could be based, from the point of view of decisions about an overall budget limit, NICE's evaluative approach is incomplete. Other technical tasks that need to be undertaken include measuring on a more systematic basis the actual health outcomes arising from health care activities, and the value society places on the benefits of major care programmes (see 'What is extra spending on the NHS producing now?').

Setting limits to spending is not just a technical matter. Within the current policy framework, key actors in the health care system and those with an interest in how NHS money is spent operate within a set of incentives which, from the point of view of health care spending, tend to add to the pressures to increase spending:

Individuals: once individuals have entered the health system their influence on the demand for health care can in turn be influenced, depending on the incentives they face.

Currently, initiatives to increase patient choice and access to health care services may be increasing public expectations of what the NHS can or should deliver, which adds to spending pressures.

Health care providers: the financial framework currently being created in the health care system rewards greater levels of activity. The mix of policies and associated rhetoric which has emerged since publication of *The NHS Plan* has not helped to promote understanding of the limits to health spending. The incentives bearing on providers must be re-considered.

Treasury: relations between the Treasury and the Department of Health (in England) are formalised through a set of public service agreements covering, broadly, goals concerning improvements in health, health care and value for money improvements. However, the Treasury should begin to ask for evidence of a quite different sort, which currently the department would find hard to provide, on the benefits and costs of the major programmes it is supporting.

Regulators: NICE (National Institute for Health and Clinical Excellence) is responsible for assessing treatments before they become available through the NHS. It therefore implicitly defines the line where spending on individual therapies is 'enough', but it currently has no remit to take into account the affordability to the NHS of its recommendations. This needs to be revised and extended.

Pharmaceutical industry: The industry is naturally keen to increase sales. The government should develop ways of working with the industry which reward health creation where there is currently no profit incentive. A greater focus on *health* (as opposed to wealth) creation would be more likely to improve the health returns (that is, the benefits) of the NHS pharmaceutical budget

Department of Health: The vast majority of private and publicly funded research and development is not devoted to cost control or the promotion of system objectives such as equity of access, but rather increases in the use of drugs and other devices or the development of new forms of treatment. To help control costs, the department should become more independent from the pharmaceutical industry (as recommended by the Health Select Committee), and strengthen its role in promoting health and regulating health care.

Despite what might now be seen to be very high levels of spending, many of these stakeholders are likely to perceive that still not enough is being spent. These perceptions can be modified, but this will require changing or limiting the scope of some policies, for example the initiatives around increasing patient choice.

Taking a broader view of setting limits, there is scope for achieving some of the benefits generated by health care by other means, in particular through activities more generally thought of as public health interventions. To achieve this, however, would require a major reorientation in the way that health policy is developed.

The future for health spending in the United Kingdom: when will enough be enough?

Over the last few years the NHS across the United Kingdom, and particularly in England, has enjoyed large increases in funding in response to public views about the need (and desire) for higher spending. But there is an obvious limit to increases that outstrip the growth of the economy. With the deferment of the 2006 spending review and the government's decision to engage in a comprehensive spending review in 2007, there is an opportunity to begin to formulate appropriate actions and policy in response to this looming spending dilemma.

The options for future NHS spending include the following:

- carry on increasing spending at current rates – that is, postpone the inevitable decision to contain spending
- carry on increased spending at current rates and improve efficiency and productivity – that is, buy extra time before confronting the inevitable decision to contain spending
- align NHS spending growth to general, long-term growth in the economy as a whole with possible adjustments to devote a modestly greater share of GDP to health care as GDP grows.

The first of these options is likely to be untenable in the medium to long run. The implied health budget would itself be hard to finance, but other programmes – including social care and pensions – are also likely to impose increased demands on the public purse.

The second represents the current position, but this is likely to be viable only for the current planning period – up to 2008.

The last of these options must be the medium to long-term goal. It is not an easy option to pursue. If the forces driving up demand and costs cannot be contained, and resistance to increased taxation reaches a critical point, then this option will also bring into sharp relief the need to be explicit about what degree of inequality in access to health care (and health) society is prepared to put up with.

Recommendations

There is a need to develop a rational, acceptable and evidence-informed process for arriving at sensible limits to health care spending without abandoning the two core equity values of the NHS: that it is funded in a progressive way (the rich contribute a higher fraction of their income than the poor) and that it is accessible at time of need regardless of non-health factors such as income, geography and so on.

Strengthening the knowledge base

How much public money should be spent on the provision of health care is ultimately a political matter. But if such decisions are to be informed by evidence of their implications, then the evidence base bearing on the benefits of additional spending will have to be strengthened. This should include:

- a programme of research to examine the benefits of each of the new policy initiatives
- quantification of the public's *valuation* of health benefits and associated benefits of health care
- systematic use of measures of the health impact of particular procedures
- an extension of the role of NICE to examine new areas of treatment and policy areas
- strengthening internal impact assessments and extending the use of evaluations.

Changing the policy framework

Given the incentives facing individuals, clinical and research professionals and the private sector, more investment will never be enough. But there is scope for modifying the current pattern of incentives so as to moderate their impact.

The Department of Health should therefore:

- ensure that the technical agenda set out in the recommendations above is actively pursued within a benefit–cost matrix (see the full paper for one example of how such a matrix could be devised)
- give up its sponsorship role for the pharmaceutical industry (as recommended by the Health Select Committee)
- ensure that the system of financial and other incentives imposed on the NHS, including its users, encourages appropriate reductions in activity while also reducing the instances of inappropriate treatment
- strengthen the role of NICE and ensure that the publicly funded research programme supports this strengthened role by providing the evidence needed for comparative evaluation of treatment options.

1 Introduction

In 2000 the UK Prime Minister Tony Blair committed the government to increasing health spending as a proportion of gross domestic product (GDP) up to the average level in the European Union (Appleby and Boyle 2000). Since then, the NHS budget has been growing at around 10 per cent a year, or about 7.5 per cent in real terms. These are unprecedented sustained growth rates that, if maintained, would mean that total spending (public plus private) on health care would, by 2008, absorb around 9.8 per cent of GDP (assuming that private spending remains constant at around 1.2 per cent of GDP). This would be equivalent to spending levels in France in 2001.

If spending increased at the same rate beyond 2008, by 2011 it would have risen to around 11 per cent of GDP – similar to German levels in 2001. In a further five or six years, total United Kingdom health care spending would reach levels similar to those currently committed by the highest spending country in the world: the United States (*see* Figure 1).

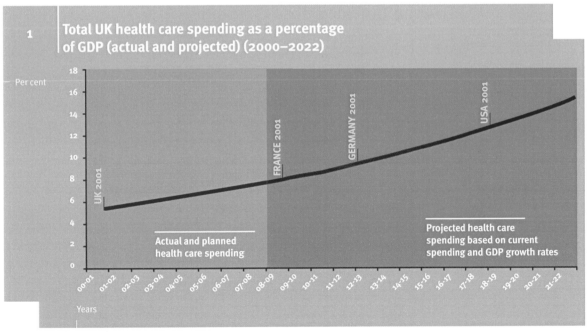

1 **Total UK health care spending as a percentage of GDP (actual and projected) (2000–2022)**

Per cent

Years

Actual and planned health care spending

Projected health care spending based on current spending and GDP growth rates

Source: Authors' calculations

The growth in health spending already committed to by the government represents a massive increase – equivalent to around 2.5 percentage points of GDP between 2000 and 2007. This increase reflects a political judgement about the kind and quality of health care the United Kingdom should have, which has been based on reports by Sir Derek Wanless and his team within the UK Treasury (Wanless 2002; 2004).

The approach taken by Wanless in suggesting a new spending path for health care was to start with a 'vision' of what a world class health care system would look like. This included very short waiting times and defined pathways of care such as those set out in the national service frameworks. He then, broadly, estimated the costs of achieving these goals. While such an approach had the merit of defining the scale of what had to be done, it suffered from three significant weaknesses:

■ First, it did not explicitly or systematically demonstrate what health benefits the additional resources proposed by the review would produce, nor whether those resources could produce more health benefits if put to other uses (although estimates of benefits in terms of lives saved for some of the components of the extra spending, for example the money to improve clinical governance, were suggested).
■ Second, it did not consider in detail whether there were other means of producing the improved health outcomes other than through the proposed extra spending. One of the options developed, termed the 'fully engaged' scenario, did suggest that a rebalancing towards public health measures would be more effective in cost and health outcome terms, but this was not investigated in depth at the time. A subsequent report (Wanless 2004) reaffirmed the potential of public health measures, but lack of evidence ruled out development of the scenario into a plan of action.
■ Third, it did not consider what would follow *after* the target performance levels had been achieved by 2022. Implicitly, meeting these targets would then mean the NHS was 'good enough'. But by then new spending pressures and opportunities will have been created, principally through the development of new medical technologies.

Beyond the 2004 spending round

For the 2004 spending round the recommendations of the first Wanless report (2002) remain in force; the existing spending plans will carry through to 2007/08. But after that, then what? Wanless suggests in two of the three future scenarios that spending should plateau at around 11 per cent of GDP by 2022. The third scenario suggests a limit of around 14 per cent after this date, but there is little justification for proposing these turning points (*see* Figure 2 opposite). Indeed, the only justification given is that by around 2022 UK health care spending will have 'caught up' with its European neighbours and that spending decisions will merely become a question of 'keeping up'.

But if health spending does not reach a plateau, by 2026 the United Kingdom could be spending one pound of every five in the economy on health care. And, stretching such projections to their limit, in 40 years' time, if growth in health care spending continues to outstrip growth in the economy, half of the nation's wealth would be spent on health care. To accommodate such spending, consumption of non-health care goods and services as a proportion of GDP would have to decline massively (although, given expansion of the economy as a whole, real expenditure in this sector would increase). Taxes would most probably have to rise (with increases ameliorated somewhat because of the larger 'tax pool') and other public services would see their share of GDP decline (although, again, real spending could still increase). Furthermore, health employment would rise substantially and productivity in the economy overall would fall as the traditionally lower levels of productivity growth of the health sector diluted higher levels in other sectors of the economy.

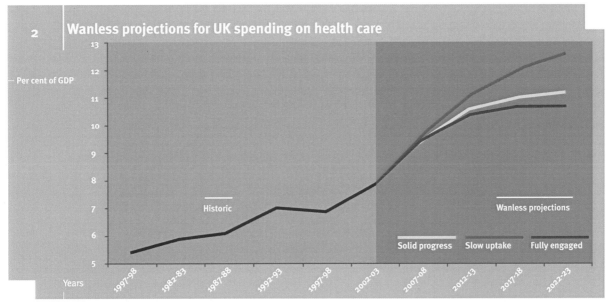

2 Wanless projections for UK spending on health care

Source: Wanless, 2000

Such projections are clearly not credible (or are they? – *see* 'Lessons from America' opposite), but they serve to make a point. Despite rising public expectations of the quality of health care and the inexorable growth in new (and generally more costly) ways of improving health-related quality and length of life through medical technology, there must inevitably come a point when we need to address the question: when is enough enough? In other words, can a limit be set to growth of health spending as a proportion of GDP? This question is likely to loom in importance as part of the 2007 comprehensive spending review when the government will have to decide if the surge in health spending should continue, and if so at what rate.

The Wanless review's answer to the precise course of future spending was to assume a period (2003/04 to 2007/08) during which health spending would 'catch up' with other European Union states. Wanless then forecast that between 2008 and 2022 spending increases would reduce but still 'keep up' with 'rising standards across all countries' (Wanless 2002, p 78).

LESSONS FROM AMERICA

Nowhere in the world is the issue of the sustainability of increased health care spending more acute than in the United States. Currently, the US share of GDP spending on health care – 13.9 per cent – is the largest in the world. Historically, growth rates have been well above that of the economy as a whole. During the 1960s and 1970s, for example, annual growth in spending averaged around 2 per cent; in the 1980s this increased to around 3.5 per cent. In the 1990s it was 1.5 per cent (Technical Review Panel on the Medicare Trustees Report 2000).

These increases may, in some respects, seem relatively small. But their implications over the long term are staggering. Estimates of future spending up to 2075 are produced by the Medicare Trustees Board (which, by law, has to report annually to Congress on the financial and actuarial status of the Old-Age, Survivors and Disability Insurance Trust Funds), with underlying models and assumptions of the trustees' reports periodically investigated by the Technical Review Panel (Technical Review Panel on the Medicare Trustees Report 2000).

The latest review of the projection models and data used by the trustees was carried out in 2000. Based on the historic record, the review details five alternative growth paths for total (not just Medicare) health care spending as a percentage of GDP (see graph below).

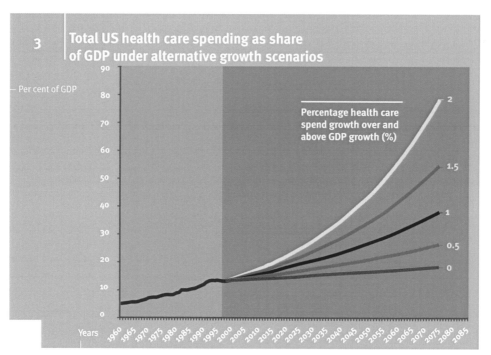

Source: Technical review panel, 2000

On these projections, if health care spending were to exceed GDP growth by 2 per cent a year – which is less than the historic average – by 2075 health care would consume 79 per cent of GDP. Even the middle-range estimate of 1 per cent excess growth would imply health care spending of 38 per cent of GDP by 2075 – a figure that the '[Technical Review] Panel does not view... as implausible' (Technical Review Panel on the Medicare Trustees Report 2000, p 39).

The review panel goes on to note the knock-on effects on the rest of the economy of such a high proportion of GDP being spent on health: non-health care consumption would fall 20 percentage points to 62 per cent of GDP (although real spending would be higher than current levels given the expansion of the whole economy); public funding of all or part of the growth would require a combination of increased taxes and individual user contributions or, potentially, legislative caps on further government outlays. Health care employment would nearly double, from 9 to 17 per cent of all jobs in the economy.

Although such international benchmarking is a perfectly acceptable pragmatic solution to the issue of deciding spending levels, it still begs the underlying question of when 'enough is enough'. In particular it ignores the possibility that the pressure to spend may continue to grow more rapidly than the projected budget could cope with. If it did, then the question would arise: should the forces making for more spending be resisted – which may or may not be politically feasible – or should they be accommodated by making more finance available, either through existing means like general taxation or in some other way?

Why does spending grow?

Any case for resisting further rapid expenditure growth rests in part on what factors are behind any push for more spending. If, for example, changes in demography were largely responsible, then it would be hard to argue that growth should be resisted – otherwise average standards of care would actually fall unless offsetting gains in efficiency could be achieved. If, on the other hand, growth was largely accounted for by improvements in the quality and effectiveness of the care available, then the question would be: what rate of improvement is it worthwhile financing?

Smith *et al* (2000) report on two attempts to estimate the contribution various factors have made to the growth in US health care spending between 1940 and 1990. Both suggest that factors such as income (personal or national), ageing populations and supplier-induced demand are probably relatively insignificant.

The low importance attached to demography runs counter to what has often been assumed in the past. The average age of the population in most countries has been rising; health spending rises with age, particularly towards the very end of life. But an increase in the general level of health has meant that most of the 'costs of dying' have been postponed and there has been an extension in the number of years of healthy life.

Numerous studies have suggested that as the average age at death has risen the associated costs have been postponed. For example, Seshamani and Gray (2004a; 2004b) found that proximity to death explained most of the increase in health spending at the end of life. The rest was due to age. Dixon *et al* (2004) found that the average number of bed days spent in hospital in the period before death does not rise with increasing age. Other work (Canadian Health Services Research Foundation 2003) reports that health care costs tend to be lower the older people are when they die, although their social care costs may be higher. This work suggests that earlier estimates of the health care costs of an ageing population considerably exaggerated the impact of demographic change.

It is actually technological change – new medicines, new surgical techniques and so on – that is identified as the dominant factor (*see* Figure 3 overleaf). Newhouse (1992) estimates that it accounted for over 65 per cent of the growth in US health spending from 1940 to 1990, while Cutler (1995) provides a lower, but still dominant, estimate of 49 per cent. On the other hand, increases in costs are also significant, reducing considerably the value of the gains from new technology. Both studies indicate, however, that income growth has been significant, suggesting that, as people become richer, they are willing to pay more for a given improvement in health. Higher costs, in other words, may be offset by increases in perceived value.

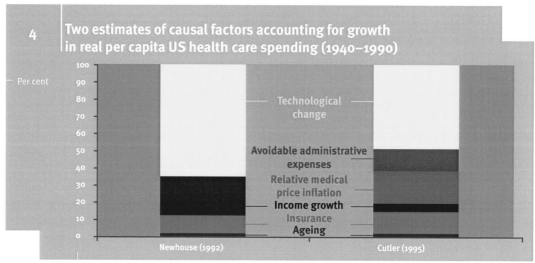

4 Two estimates of causal factors accounting for growth in real per capita US health care spending (1940–1990)

Per cent

Technological change

Avoidable administrative expenses

Relative medical price inflation

Income growth

Insurance

Ageing

Newhouse (1992)

Cutler (1995)

Source: Newhouse (1992) and Cutler (1995)

The accuracy of these estimates is hard to judge. What is even harder to assess is the impact future technological development will have on health care spending. New medical technologies can open up new areas for medical intervention. These technologies may reduce or increase costs. However, the net impact of technological development on the costs of health care has been the major driver for increased health care spending, at least historically, as both Newhouse (1992) and Cutler (1995) suggest.

So, should the NHS budget be allowed to keep on expanding to keep up with such technical advances, even if this is beyond average growth in GDP? If not, what justification can be provided for limiting funding?

Why limit spending?

For most goods and services this question would not arise. No one would argue for limiting spending on any other consumable good, from televisions to cabbages. This argument holds for all those forms of health care spending that people meet themselves (such as over-the-counter drugs). If, for example, individuals want more analgesics because they are less tolerant of pain than they used to be, and they bear the costs of such demand themselves, then their spending decision is theirs alone. The decision they take will be one in which they will (at least in theory) balance the benefits and costs of their purchase of analgesics against the alternative benefits they have had to forgo. This, in essence, is an unavoidable (and unexceptional) rationing decision performed in private markets.

It does not, however, hold to the same degree for publicly financed health care. In this case those who pay for health care (taxpayers) are not, at any particular point in time, the same as those who use the services financed in this way. In a system like the NHS the state must in effect act as a 'guardian' for taxpayers, ensuring that the funds diverted from personal use to health care are sufficient for the purpose that is intended, and that they are used wisely.

Putting the health care budget to the vote

Imagine if taxpayers could vote specifically on how much should be spent on health care. If such a vote were possible, what kind of arguments would be relevant to inform voters' decisions? Voters might wish to set limits on health care spending for three reasons.

First, some kinds of spending might be judged unethical – some advances in reproductive technology such as human cloning perhaps fall into this category. Some of the purposes of health spending may be questioned: Hanson and Callahan (1999) consider the case for using medical knowledge to enhance 'natural' human characteristics. They argue that (p 12):

> ... while believing it neither possible nor desirable to attempt to outlaw efforts to 'enhance' natural human characteristics, we find considerable wariness and scepticism in order. There is little solid knowledge on which to base efforts to improve or enhance our nature, no consensus on what would count as enhancement, and little basis whatever for knowing whether the long-term genetic or social consequences would be good or bad.

Second, some kinds of spending, such as cosmetic surgery, may be considered ethical but not suitable for public subsidy and hence not classified as health care. However, there are no clear-cut criteria for determining what is or is not health care. In the recent past, dentistry and long-term care have hovered on the borderline but remain at least in part under the NHS banner. Now, complementary medicines, 'healthy' foods and activities such as systematic exercise are emerging as potential candidates for extending the scope of publicly funded health care. Changes to the licensing of medicines, which are allowing an increasing number of drugs to be sold over the counter, work the other way by transferring their cost to the budgets of the people paying for them.

Third, the benefits of additional spending may be judged not sufficient to justify the transfer of funds from personal to public use. Although more spending on health arising from the introduction of new medical technologies may provide some benefits, these may be outweighed by the benefits of putting that money to other uses – in other words, the opportunity costs of providing them are too great. This case for focusing on the relationship between (financial) inputs and (health) outcomes has been made by others (for example Propper 2001).

This approach has already been adopted by the NHS. For example, in the 1990s, a number of items that had been prescribed up until then ceased to be available within the NHS; for example, many cough remedies were judged to be clinically ineffective and taken off prescribing lists. They remain available for individuals to buy out of their own resources.

Subsequently this process was put on a more systematic footing with the establishment of the National Institute for Clinical Excellence (NICE) in 1999 (this became the National Institute for Health and Clinical Excellence in 2005, although it is still known as NICE). NICE collects and reviews the evidence on the value of new drugs and other forms of treatment and issues advice to the NHS as to whether these drugs or other therapies should be used. So far it has made very few recommendations to exclude the interventions it has considered, but it has suggested both that restrictions be placed on some forms of treatment and that cheaper forms of treatment be used where more expensive ones are judged to provide little or no extra benefit.

About this paper

The remainder of this paper will focus on the third argument presented above. In doing so, it asks the question: what is the point at which the benefits of additional spending may be judged not sufficient to justify the transfer of funds from personal to public use? This is not to suggest that growth in the NHS budget beyond the levels currently allowed for would be unsustainable (*see* Annexe 1). However, it does raise the question of whether there is ultimately a limit to the amount that can be spent on health – a point when 'enough is enough'.

2 The economics of health spending

Spending on health, as on any other good, is worthwhile as long as the benefits it brings exceed those that could be obtained by other forms of spending. Implicit in the rise in spending noted earlier is the judgement that, despite the increases that have already occurred in health spending, the benefits continue to be greater in health care than in other possible uses.

However, the usual assumption is that as spending in a particular area rises there will inevitably come a point where the benefits at the margin will tend to fall. It might also be possible for the absolute benefits to fall as spending increases still further (*see* Figure 5 overleaf).

Health spending: the relationship between costs and benefits

There is no reason why health should be an exception to this assumption. At low levels of spending the most productive activities (in terms of 'healthiness'), such as immunisation and vaccination, along with basic primary care and the most cost-effective drugs, will be financed. As spending rises it will tend to be devoted to activities and treatments that, while beneficial, yield less in terms of direct health benefits as conventionally measured by, for example, reductions in mortality or increases in life expectancy. They may of course produce other benefits such as convenience of access, a more pleasant care process and so on.

However, the 'returns curve' set out in Figure 4 is not static and changes over time, for four main reasons:

- the cost of provision may rise or fall so that at every level of spending, more (or fewer) net benefits are produced
- the nature and extent of ill health in the population may rise, increasing the need for treatment and the potential benefits from spending more
- the 'value' attached to health benefits may change for a variety of reasons
- new treatments may be introduced due to technical change – while some may reduce the cost of treatment, others may extend its scope.

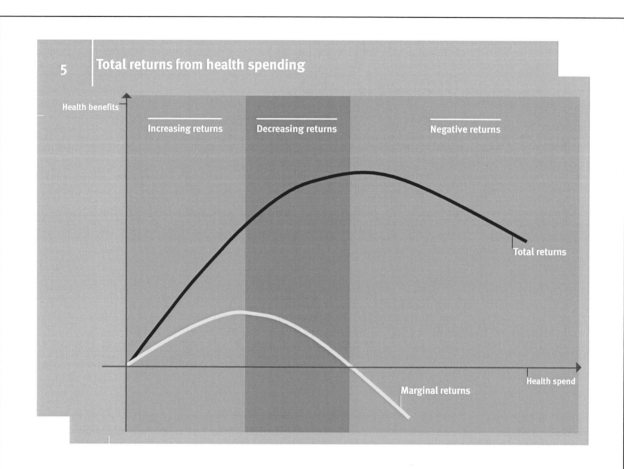

5 | **Total returns from health spending**

Health benefits

Increasing returns | Decreasing returns | Negative returns

Total returns

Marginal returns

Health spend

It should be noted that the optimal level of health care spending is *not* necessarily at the point where the total returns curve peaks (and marginal returns are zero). The point at which spending on health care ceases to become a good investment depends on the returns (not necessarily measured in terms of health benefits) to be derived from switching spending to other things such as education, housing or private spending.

Determining the optimal level of health care spending (that is, the point at which 'allocative efficiency' is maximised) would require the Herculean task of quantifying (in commensurate units) *all* the total returns curves for *all* possible uses of the nation's scarce resources across *all* levels of spending, and then allocating resources (in effect setting budgets) for *every* possible type of spending in a way that maximised returns at every level of spending until all resources are consumed. This exercise would need to be undertaken continuously to accommodate technological changes. The fact that every individual would place different values on the returns from different types of spending adds an almost infinitely complicating twist to an already near-impossible task. It is perhaps no surprise, therefore, that the economist's traditional preferred allocative/rationing mechanism is the market. However, Chapter 4 of this paper will consider attempts to replace this mechanism.

Figure 6 opposite shows how increased health care spending can be viewed as worthwhile *if* the returns to investment curve shifts upwards as a result of the factors noted above and, importantly, given the starting position in terms of spending and resultant health benefits.

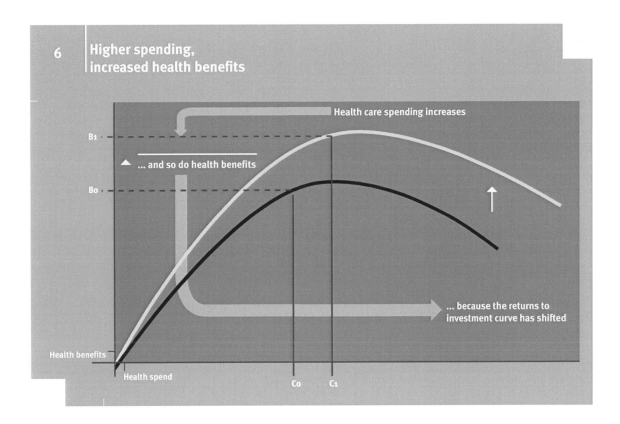

The following three sections examine each of the three parts of the returns curve: where returns are strongly positive, where they start to decline and where they become negative.

Positive returns for health

In most of the developed world, life expectancy has grown steadily – with brief interruptions – for more than the last hundred years. At the same time, but particularly since the end of the Second World War, so too has spending on health. These two facts represent prima facie evidence that the returns from health spending have been positive for most if not all of this period.

However, while health, in terms of life expectancy, has improved throughout the last century, and been maintained during the lifetime of the NHS (*see* Figure 7 overleaf), it is not obvious how much of this can be properly attributed to the expansion in health care.

At one extreme is the argument associated with Thomas McKeown (1979). In this view, most of the improvement in health cannot be attributed to the expansion of health care services and new drugs because improvements started before these were introduced. Instead, improvements in income and social capital (particularly education) have been the main determinants driving gains in health.

Critics of this thesis (such as Szreter 2000) have argued that McKeown overplayed the role of income growth and underplayed the effect of public health measures during the 19th century. Others believe that while McKeown's thesis was correct for approximately the first half of the 20th century (during which time doctors had few effective drugs at their

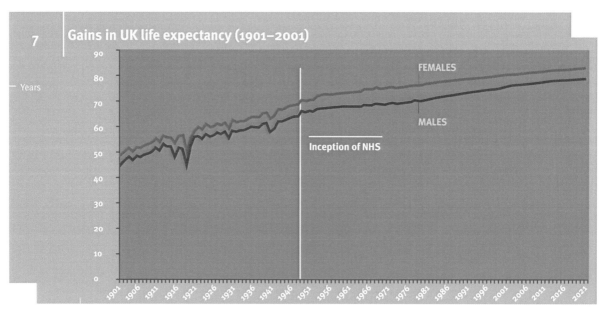

7 **Gains in UK life expectancy (1901–2001)**

Years

FEMALES

MALES

Inception of NHS

Source: Government actuary's department

disposal), the extensive innovation in drugs and surgical procedures over the past 50 years has meant that the contribution of health care to health has steadily increased (Bunker 2001).

How great has this been? There are no conclusive studies that unambiguously pin down the contribution of the different factors that determine life expectancy, taking the full spectrum of diseases with which health care deals. A number of studies have aimed to identify and isolate the contribution of specific health interventions. These demonstrate, with varying degrees of reliability, that health care spending has produced significant benefits for particular conditions.

Mackenbach (1996), for example, reworked McKeown's argument and concluded that medical care had made only a limited contribution (less than 20 per cent) to the decline in mortality up to 1970, but a much greater one after that. However, as he points out, there are weaknesses in the calculations, of which perhaps the most important is the assumption of a direct causation between the availability of an effective medical treatment and any subsequent improvement in health.

In some cases this is clearly an appropriate assumption to make. For example, Bunker (2001) makes estimates of the gains from a number of surgical interventions such as cataract removal and hip replacement which deal with conditions that are not self-limiting if left untreated (*see also* Albert *et al* 1996). But in other cases it is not clear that this is the case. For ischaemic heart disease, thrombolytic therapy has saved lives. However, as Mackenbach acknowledges, it cannot be demonstrated conclusively using the available data that *all* recent declines in mortality from this disease derive *solely* from this medical intervention.

Cutler and Kadiyala (1999) have attempted to disentangle the impact of medical interventions on cardiovascular disease from other sources of life extension. They estimate that one-third of recent reductions in deaths from cardiovascular disease could be attributed to better acute care, one-third from increased use of better medicines and one-third to behavioural change (p 156). Even if these estimates are only approximately correct they suggest that medical care produces a reasonable return on investment.

As these and other authors point out, the value of the extension of life and improvement in its quality is so great that, even if medical interventions were responsible for only a small fraction of the total observed improvements in life expectancy, in all likelihood that would be sufficient to justify them. For example, Nordhaus (2003) states that (p 35):

> ... to a first approximation, the economic value of increases in longevity in the last 100 years is about as large as the value of measured growth in non-health goods and services.

Even if this argument is accepted, however, it may still be the case that spending on health care has now reached the flatter (that is, decreasing marginal returns) part of the curve. What evidence is there to support this view?

Declining returns for health

In a recent review of the contribution of health care to health, Nolte and McKee (2004) investigate the concept of 'avoidable mortality' (that is, deaths that could be avoided given appropriate access to prevailing medical technology). They estimate the contribution to increased life expectancy across selected countries in Europe of mortality changes in conditions amenable to care. These were selected on the basis of evidence that health care was the cause of reduced mortality and hence, they assumed, acted as indicators of the impact of health care on life expectancy. Their results for the United Kingdom (see Figure 8 overleaf) suggest that the contribution of amenable conditions to changes in life expectancy over the period 1980–89 for men (an increase in life expectancy of 1.3 years) and women (an increase in life expectancy of 0.8 years) was around 37 per cent and 57.5 per cent respectively. However, for the period 1990–1998, these contributions fell to 15.6 per cent and 42.8 per cent for increases in life expectancy of one year for men, and 0.6 years for women.

These results suggest that, while still positive, the contribution of health care to life expectancy is diminishing. Interestingly, as Figure 8 shows, reduced mortality from ischaemic heart disease (IHD) contributed significantly to increases in life expectancy for both men and women. However, the causes of the reduction in IHD mortality are not completely known, and can be only partly attributed to health care.

The evidence for pharmaceuticals

In recent years many evaluations of the impact of new drugs have been carried out. In England, NICE has evaluated a number of drugs that could be regarded as 'marginal' within the NHS because they are just becoming available or because their use has been restricted until now. These have generally been found to be 'value for money' and hence have been recommended for general use. However, few provide massive benefits: rather, they extend quality and length of life by small amounts.

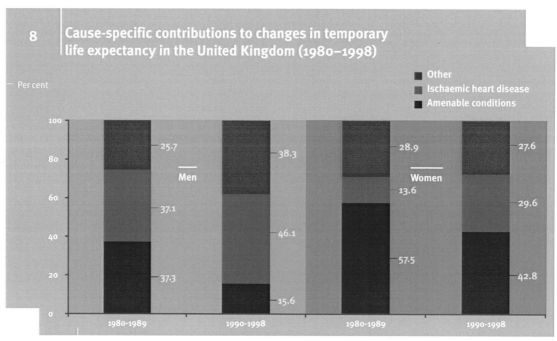

8 | **Cause-specific contributions to changes in temporary life expectancy in the United Kingdom (1980–1998)**

Per cent

- Other
- Ischaemic heart disease
- Amenable conditions

Men: 1980-1989: 25.7, 37.1, 37.3; 1990-1998: 38.3, 46.1, 15.6

Women: 1980-1989: 28.9, 13.6, 57.5; 1990-1998: 27.6, 29.6, 42.8

Source: Nolte and Mckee, 2004

Furthermore, NICE's evaluations do not and cannot take into account the gains actually achieved in day-to-day use. Here, other factors may come into play, such as low rates of compliance, which will tend to depress the level of benefits actually achieved.

A number of other findings support the view that the value of the drugs now coming on to the market is declining. Lichtenberg (2003) found that the impact of new drugs has been diminishing: in the most recent time period studied, a 10 per cent increase in new drug approvals produced a 5 per cent reduction in mortality, much lower than in previous years.

There are also signs of diminishing marginal productivity in the search for better treatments, and hence a rising marginal cost of new discoveries (at least in the drug field). Expenditure on pharmaceutical research in the United Kingdom and worldwide has been growing steadily, particularly within the private sector, but the results have proved disappointing.

Taylor (2003), for example, refers to a worldwide crisis in productivity in pharmaceutical research. He argues that (p 408):

> ... the reasons behind such trends range from tighter regulation to the inherently complex nature of modern research in areas such as oncology, neurology and virology. For example, unavoidable technical reasons may exist so that tomorrow's new pharmaceuticals will – unlike present blockbusters such as the statins, cyclo-oxygenase-2 inhibitors and selective serotonin reuptake inhibitors – be products with a relatively high cost for low volumes that unlike 'blockbusters' are tailored to the needs of well defined relatively small groups.

This conclusion chimes with Le Fanu's (1999) argument that the golden age of medicine is over. The easiest challenges have now been overcome. The accidental discovery of antibiotics, for example, can be regarded as a piece of good fortune, which is unlikely to be repeated. Now, the benefits of new discoveries are much more limited. As Freemantle and Hill (2002) point out (p 865):

> ... most treatments that are intended to prevent disease, if they work at all, have only a modest impact on major morbidity and mortality. The increasing number of patients included in the clinical trials of statins bears testament to the increasingly small treatment effects that are of interest.

The impression given in the media is quite different. But as Melzer and Zimmern (2002) put it (p 864):

> ... the enormous investments needed to exploit genetics may have driven a more exuberant set of claims than usual, designed to appeal not only to the public but also to investors. Each new technology brings a crop of exaggerated claims.

Recent reports on returns from research into new drugs and the state of the pharmaceutical and biotechnology industries provide clear evidence that the marginal cost of new discoveries is rising (Jack and Bowe 2005), with the implication that although more effective drugs may be developed they will not be as cost-effective as earlier drugs. As Taylor (2003) points out, they will also be less likely to find the mass markets that have underpinned the industry's growth in the past.

Although there have been improvements in the methods used to select drugs for development prior to testing on animals and humans, these have not been significant enough to counter the forces that contribute to higher costs such as more stringent regulation. This suggests that the scope for new cost-effective health spending based on new drug technologies will be much less than is commonly assumed. Gains will continue to be made, but they will either be small gains – or small chances of a gain – for a large number of people, or substantial gains, where effective treatments are found for rare conditions, for a few. However, the introduction of other new technologies, for example new surgical techniques, is unlikely to be affected by these factors.

Negative returns for health

In Figure 5 (see p 10), the spend–benefit curve flattens out as spending rises. If this is indeed the case, as some of the evidence cited above suggests, there comes a point – even where benefits are still rising – when the extra spending will not be deemed 'worthwhile'. How that point should be defined is considered in Chapter 4.

But could the curve actually turn downwards? Could increased spending actually reduce the *total* level or value of health benefits?

There are several arguments which suggest that returns might be, or might become, negative. For example, new health care technologies can be very complex, not just for patients who may experience possible increases in the rates of non-compliance, but also for professionals, who may have a higher propensity to make mistakes when delivering treatments.

Fisher and Welch (1999) point to:

> ... the numerous steps required at each phase of common treatments: anticoagulation, including initiating, dispensing, monitoring, and adjusting therapy; or a laparoscopic cholecystectomy, including preparing the equipment, anesthetizing the patient, carrying out the procedure itself, and following up with postoperative care. Even if the probability of failure in any single step is low (e.g. 1%), the probability of at least 1 failure rises with the number of steps (e.g. with 10 steps the probability is 10%; with 100 steps the probability is 63%; with 1000 steps the probability exceeds 99.9%). As there is more to do, systems become more complex and mistakes are more likely. (p 451)

Until recently, the risks implicit in hospital treatment were largely ignored. But as a result of a series of studies, the risks inherent in the use of drugs or in hospital treatment are now well researched. Even in systems acknowledged as being well-resourced, the error rate in hospitals is high at least in part because of the complexity of those institutions and of the technologies they employ. In the words of an Institute of Medicine study (2001, p 26), 'as clinical science continues to advance, the challenge of managing the use of existing and new pharmaceutical and health technologies will intensify'.

An Institute of Medicine study published in 2000 reported on a number of research findings that showed how dangerous health care could be to patients. In 1993 medication errors alone were estimated to lead to about 7,000 deaths in the United States. Between 44,000 and 98,000 Americans die in hospitals each year as a result of all forms of medical errors. In the community, there is substantial evidence of harm resulting to older patients in particular from the complex prescribing regimes that have resulted from the availability of a wider range of drugs (Wolman and Manor 2004).

Evidence presented by Wolman and Manor suggest that the error rate in some parts of the health care system has been rising. They conclude (p 8) that 'the quality of medical services in developed countries is on a downward slope'. Put differently, even if the potential returns are rising because of new technology, the gains that are actually achieved may be falling.

The establishment of the National Patient Safety Agency and other measures to improve procedures within hospitals and other parts of the health care system indicate that there is scope for reducing errors – but at a cost that will reduce the return at the margin.

There are also many well-documented instances of treatments that were once thought to be beneficial, but which turn out to be harmful (for example, thalidomide and contamination of human growth hormone, and the use of albumen on burns) (McKee 1999). However, whether such instances go up as total spending increases is not clear; it is perhaps more likely that spending on the 'wrong' interventions can occur at any given level of financing if they are introduced without proper evaluation of their effects.

International comparisons: confusing evidence for the returns-to-investment curve?

Comparisons between countries spending different amounts on health reveal confusing conclusions. If there are diminishing marginal returns to health spending at any given level of technology, then this should be apparent in the overall health of countries spending

Figure 9 suggests a relationship between health spending and life expectancy that is positive, but which declines overall as spending rises. However, it is clear that the implicit model on which this result is based – that life expectancy is solely a function of health spending – is too simple. For example, the United States spends five times more on health care than the Republic of Korea yet achieves only the same average level of life expectancy. Similarly, Cuba and Swaziland spend similar amounts on health care yet life expectancy in the former is nearly 90 per cent higher than in the latter. However, in terms of length of life, it would appear that there is some evidence that large gains can be made at relatively low levels of health care spending (up to around US$600 per head), but that beyond this gains are much smaller. Nevertheless, this is not necessarily an argument for high spending countries to reduce spending on health care as such countries may value what gains are achieved more highly or concentrate on other benefits such as improvements in health-related quality of life and the process (as opposed to the outcome) of care.

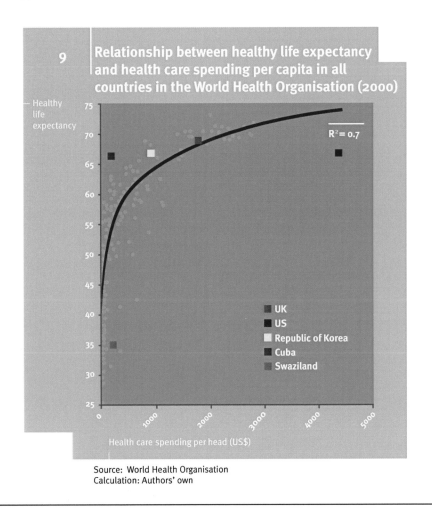

9 Relationship between healthy life expectancy and health care spending per capita in all countries in the World Health Organisation (2000)

$R^2 = 0.7$

Healthy life expectancy

■ UK
■ US
□ Republic of Korea
■ Cuba
■ Swaziland

Health care spending per head (US$)

Source: World Health Organisation
Calculation: Authors' own

different amounts of money per capita. In industrialised countries, more or less the same technologies are in universal use, delivered in similar if not identical ways, and hence the higher levels of spending in some countries should be producing a modest return. If the higher spending is not producing a markedly improved health performance that would suggest that returns are declining at the margin.

However, the evidence from international cross-sectional studies and time series analyses of health spending is not clear-cut.

There is evidence to suggest that, while there appears to be a relationship between health care spending and various measures of health (such as life expectancy), returns do not grow proportionately. Figure 9 (*see* p 17), for example, suggests a fairly strong (non-linear) relationship between health and health care spending. Assuming the direction of causation is from spending to health it is possible, depending on the starting position for a country, to make a rough calculation of the returns to increased spending in terms of life expectancy. For example, in Mozambique a US$10 increase in health care spending per capita could improve average life expectancy by 1.2 years (to 43.9 years). For the United Kingdom, however, the same increase in per capita spending would produce an added average life expectancy of just two weeks.

Of course, these calculations are based on a very simplistic model, with life expectancy being solely a function of health care spending. And, as Figure 9 also shows, there are some wide variations in the data – represented by the fitted curve – which the model fails to explain.

Clearly, the financial inputs to health care services are only one of a number of factors determining population health measures such as healthy life expectancy; from a false premise (or a simplistic, under- or mis-specified model) any conclusion is possible. For example, as Joseph Newhouse (1977) demonstrated nearly 30 years ago, the level of a country's health care spending is associated with a country's level of wealth or GDP (*see* Figure 10, below). In economic terms health care is a 'luxury good' which increasingly

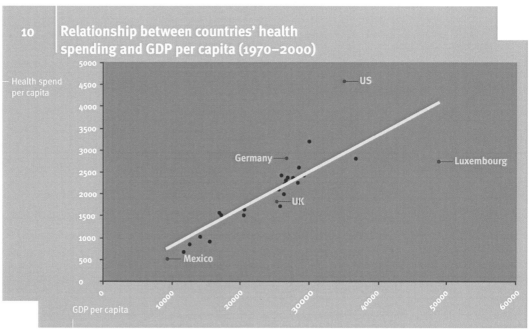

Source: OECD Health data file 2004
Calculation: Authors' own

becomes the purchase of choice as a country's wealth goes up. And, through a variety of non-health care mechanisms, as wealth increases so too does health.

But numerous cross-country studies of the determinants of health suggest that while the 'wealth variable', such as per capita GDP, tends to be positively correlated with health, virtually all permutations of health care spending (share of GDP, per capita spend and so on) tend to contribute little to explaining variations in countries' health. In any case they are, by and large, statistically non-significant anyway (see Kwangkee and Moody 1992; Hertz et al 1994; Filmer and Pritchett 1999).

This statistical story gets more confusing as yet other studies suggest that health care spending is an important and significant factor in explaining variations in health across countries and regions and over time. Wang (2002) shows that for 60 low income countries, health share of GDP (although interestingly not per capita health care spend) is significant. Wolfe's (1986) analysis of six developed countries supports this view, arguing that there is a positive link between health care expenditure and health, but that (p 998) 'this says nothing about whether money is better spent influencing lifestyle… or medical expenditures'.

An attempt to tease out factors has been made by a more recent 'production function' study by Or (2001) of 21 OECD countries. Or used non-monetary measures of health care supply together with other health care and non-health care variables to explain variations in a number of population health measures. She showed that health care (doctors per 1000 population), institutional factors (for example, the existence of gate-keeping) and non-health care variables (such as GDP per capita) were all positively associated with health.

And yet, as Jones (2002) notes, examining changes in life expectancy versus changes in health care's share of GDP across countries, there is very little association to be observed.

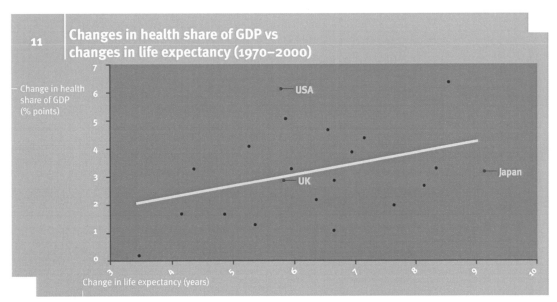

11 | **Changes in health share of GDP vs changes in life expectancy (1970–2000)**

Source: OECD Health data file
Calculations: Authors' own

Figure 11 updates Jones' data from 1960–1997 to 1970–2000: this shows a very weak but non-significant association.

These findings suggest that the confused relationship may in part be explained by differences in the health care policies pursued by different countries. In some respects, high spending countries may be regarded as wasteful and inefficient. Examples of this could include the relatively high levels of spending on drugs in France, or comparatively large medical salaries in the United States as well as higher absolute levels of inappropriate care. In other words, they may be spending 'too much' if the opportunity costs of the extra spending were properly identified and taken into account.

Miller and Frech (2000) find that more spending on drugs is linked to better health, confirming a number of studies by Lichtenberg (2001) which suggest a link between the introduction of new drugs and improved life expectancy as well as other benefits such as increased employment. But Miller's work suggests that French (and Italian) spending on drugs is such that they have little to benefit from increasing their consumption. In contrast, other countries currently spending much less stand to gain considerably more. With respect to non-pharmaceutical health care spending, however, Miller and Frech conclude that in all developed countries such spending has virtually no effect on life expectancy at birth. They suggest that this 'could indicate that developed countries are on the flat of the curve when it comes to non-pharmaceutical health care consumption', although they go on to add that this may be a statistical artefact resulting from the links between spending, national wealth and health.

The United States has the largest per capita spend (some of which is due to higher relative factor costs) and a high rate of medical interventions (in most areas) compared to the United Kingdom. A series of RAND studies has found that about one-third or more of all procedures performed in the United States are of questionable benefit (McGlynn 1998). Similarly, a series of studies by Wennberg (2004) of the health implications of different spending levels in US states found no correlation between spending and health, or even between spending and patient satisfaction. Some of this research suggests that returns are negative in high spending states. According to Wennberg this is in part because the higher intensity treatments available result in patients being given care that they would choose not to have if choice were available (for example, towards the end of their lives). In other words, higher levels of spending reflect the priorities of the providers and the incentives they are faced with, not patients' views of the likely benefits of treatment.

However, another study (McGlynn et al 2003) found widespread evidence of under-treatment in the United States. Reviewing the management of 30 common conditions, the study concluded that the people surveyed received only 55 per cent of recommended care. The shortfalls were greater for some conditions than others, but nevertheless they were identified across all main health services including prevention and screening.

How these two findings 'balance out' is uncertain, but the implication is clear: a country may reach a point on the curve where marginal benefits from some forms of health spending are falling for some of its citizens at the same time as they are still rising for others. If this is generally true then country-level studies are of limited value: studies of individual drugs or procedures, particularly those coming into use, may be of more value.

Summary of international evidence

Inter-country comparisons that measure the actual *return* to investment have tended to focus on outcomes such as mortality or life expectancy because these are routinely measured. However, they have ignored other valid reasons for investment that are not routinely measured, such as improvements in quality of life or the process of health care.

What has been established is that a country's health is intimately and positively linked with its wealth in two senses. First, higher levels of fairly distributed GDP imply better standards of living – better housing, nutrition, education, environmental infrastructure and so on – which contribute to improvements in population health (although it remains an open question as to what degree of distribution of any given total of GDP best maximises health effects). Second, as GDP goes up, spending on health care is increasingly favoured over other uses of resources.

As Bengt Jonsson has pointed out, just because health spending is statistically associated with GDP, this does not necessarily mean that countries above or below the line of best fit (*see* Figure 10, p 18) should aim to bring their spending literally 'into line'. In other words, the apparent relationship between wealth and health spending alone does not provide a normative rule to guide decisions about health care spending. Hence, the reasons for this relationship need to be better understood.

In fact, on some measures, the link between income and health spending is weak – that is, demand is not elastic (Newhouse 1992). Further, as income rises, the expectation would be that the average level of health would also rise and the need for health spending would diminish. The main reason this has not occurred has been the introduction of new forms of treatment which, although 'expensive', are more effective and hence reduce the cost of care (when standardised for outcome) (Jones 2002).

It follows that there is no direct (or at least straightforward) mechanism that links health spending to GDP. Rather, all industrialised countries have experienced similar technology changes and reacted in more or less the same way.

Future value of marginal benefits

This paper's initial presumption – that as spending rises the *rate* of increase in the value of benefits goes down – may have been justified to now. But there are several reasons why this evidence may be misleading as a guide to future levels of spending.

New technology

The evidence presented above has suggested that new technology has been the main driver for more spending in the past. Although its impact may be declining, the reasons for scepticism set out earlier may prove to be wrong, and new areas for clinically effective treatment may emerge. There is a massive worldwide research effort designed to produce new treatments so there can be no doubt that they will continue to emerge. What is less clear is whether or not they will prove to be cost effective.

Changing preferences

Even without technical change the benefits curve may move upwards for a number of related reasons.

As incomes rise, so too might the *value* placed on health and the *disvalue* placed on illness. According to Hall and Jones (2004), the rise in health spending in recent decades can be explained as a rational and predictable response to rising incomes. Other forms of expenditure are subject to falling marginal utility as income rises, but with health the situation is reversed. The value attached to life rises with time, and with it the value attached to services that extend it.

At the same time, it can be argued that the disvalue attached to the *consequences* of actual or perceived ill health also rises. The growth in use of health services since the foundation of the NHS does suggest that for any given degree of illness people are more inclined to seek professional help. This might be because they are less tolerant of pain and discomfort or because their expectations of what can be achieved through health care (and the circumstances in which they receive care) have risen, in part driven by the fact that more can be done.

Other sources of benefit

So far this paper's assumption has been that the benefits of extra health spending should show themselves through increased life expectancy or reductions in illness. But there are other forms of health benefits, for example reductions in pain and disability, and other types of benefits, such as easier and more convenient access, which might justify the rising levels of expenditure.

Some of these are captured in a selection of the micro-studies cited above of particular procedures or drugs, for example the benefits of greater mobility or improved sight made possible by new surgical techniques. Other benefits are not. For example, there are at least four ways in which one country might spend more than another on health without this being used for procedures or drugs.

First, the extra spending may go on improving quality of life; mental health spending is one example where resources tend to be devoted to improving quality rather than length of life (Nolte and McKee 2004).

Second, it might go on improving access to health in terms of convenience and timeliness. For example, over the last few years considerable resources in the English NHS have been devoted to reducing waiting times. While many patients benefiting from this priority will have enjoyed longer lengths of life, in specialties such as trauma and orthopaedics there is evidence that the biggest increases in volumes of treatment have been in traditionally long-wait procedures such as primary hip and knee replacements. These are operations that tend to improve quality rather than length of life (Appleby *et al* 2004a).

Third, the extra resources may be used to treat patients where the chances of success are low but still positive.

Finally, it might be used to retain larger margins of spare capacity in order, for example, to better meet peaks in demand or to cater for greater patient choice.

Spending in all these areas will produce benefits but have little impact on mortality and life expectancy or indeed reductions in disability or ill health.

In addition, there may well be non-health benefits arising from health interventions that may justify increased health spending. For example, public spending in one area (such as incapacity benefit) may be reduced by spending on health care (for example mental health services).

There appears to be no studies that aim to identify the link between spending growth and the type of health or other benefit that extra spending produces in both rich and poor countries. At low levels of spending and GDP per head, the economic benefit may be high – that is, the value of the extra contribution to GDP of a healthier workforce will make the investment in health care worthwhile. At higher levels, it is likely that benefits of convenience and other quality factors unrelated to health itself or the contribution to general economic activity that impacts on GDP become more important.

Cross-national comparisons (*see* Figure 11, p 19) suggest that high spending countries gain little in terms of life expectancy from increased spending and, instead, resources are used to make access more convenient. For example, high spending countries such as Germany and the United States allow patients to seek specialist advice directly, a 'right' that raises spending (OECD 2001). Similarly, waiting for hospital treatment is rare in these countries, even though the health benefits of reducing already short times to nearly zero are modest for all but the most urgent conditions.

Such improved access may, however, be highly valued by those who can afford to pay for it. In Fogel's words (2004, p 103):

> ... *every substantial suburban community in the United States demands its own [hospital] facility with a wide range of services.*

In other words, at the high income levels that the United States enjoys, convenience and easy access to specialists, as well as primary care physicians, form an essential part of a 'good' health care system in their own right. Their contribution to health is irrelevant.

New health problems

There may be new or increased health problems – new infectious diseases (HIV/AIDS is the classic case) or the 'wrong' social trends (for example, obesity or drug abuse) – that create new or expanded needs for treatment.

There is undoubtedly scope for 'new' health problems to emerge. The recent increases in obesity threaten to lead to large increases in demand for existing services such as diabetic care. The incidence of sexually transmitted diseases and allergies is rising and the threat of old or new infectious diseases of other kinds is increasingly being recognised.

Advances in medical technology

The last and most difficult factor to assess is change in medical technology. There are grounds for thinking that progress may be slowing, but at the same time new discoveries are announced daily which it is claimed may transform treatment of a particular disease or prevent it developing in the first place. The granting of permission to the University of

Newcastle to carry out embryo cloning in support of stem-cell research is the latest example, which may lead to a host of new treatment but few new treatments have so far been developed. That was also the expectation when the human genome was first mapped.

There is no value in attempting to come to a clear view one way or the other since the results of research are inherently unpredictable. However, given the massive effort devoted worldwide to health research, it would be surprising if the number of available and effective health care technologies did not increase even if at a slower rate than in the past. The important thing, as the next chapter will argue, is to have the means available to determine when and how the results of research and technological development *should* influence health care spending.

Overview

This brief review of some of the studies examining the returns on health care investment suggests that health spending has produced a positive return as measured by a variety of health outcomes – life expectancy, reduced mortality and so on. But, as spending rises, the rate of health returns tends to fall.

It is also clear that there are statistical limits in two areas. First, it is difficult to disentangle the determinants of observed changes in health. Second, there are problems with establishing the marginal product of health care (and how this might be changing over time).

Intervention studies – such as technology assessments carried out by NICE and some of the 'inventory' approaches by researchers like Bunker (2001) – attempt to incorporate the quality of life dimension through, for example, weights used to calculate quality-adjusted life years (QALYs). However, no study to date has managed a comprehensive and unambiguous assessment of the total returns to health care investment, including all sources of benefit and disbenefit.

This review also suggests that it is unsafe to assume that 'more means better'. Developments in health care bring disbenefits as well as benefits and it becomes an empirical question whether, at the margin, the former outweigh the latter. At any point in time, there will be examples of treatments being offered that provide little benefit. The key question is whether there is a systematic tendency to 'overshoot' across the whole field of health care.

The development of evidence-based practice and the establishment of institutions such as NICE can be seen as a recognition that more is not necessarily better. But such institutional innovations address only some of the risks identified above. Those which stem from the way users and health professionals actually behave, rather than the merits or demerits on particular technologies judged in trial conditions, require different measures.

In summary:

- there is good evidence that health services have delivered significant health gains in the recent past but the rate of improvement appears to be declining
- for a variety of reasons, extra health spending may not result in better health
- health expenditures produce other forms of benefit and these may increase more rapidly than health benefits as incomes and health spending rise
- everything else being equal, increases in the *value* society attaches to the benefits produced by health care – life years, QALYs, speedy access and so on – may explain or justify increased spending on health care.

3 What is extra spending on the NHS producing now?

So far this paper has established that the links between extra spending and health, and benefits of other kinds, are complex, ranging from strongly positive to negative. The general presumption of the argument set out here is that, in the absence of major technological change, benefits will be strongly positive for low and medium levels of spending. They will decline at the margin as spending rises to the highest levels currently being adopted in industrialised countries.

As the United Kingdom has been a low spender relative to other countries in Western Europe, the expectation might be that at current levels of spending returns would be high, but as spending rises towards the EU average – which it will do in the near future – they would begin to tail off, at least in terms of benefits to health.

The first Wanless report (2002) argued that a large increase in resources was required if the NHS was to provide a 'good enough' service, but this was largely defined by what it could *provide* rather than by what *health gain* – or any other kind of benefit – it would generate.

The government itself has not attempted to define what the extra spending is likely to produce in terms of health or any other benefits. The NHS Plan (Department of Health 2000a) defined service objectives, such as reducing waiting times, and other changes that are justified only partly in terms of health benefits, for example expanding patient choice of hospital or the establishment of walk-in centres. In some areas, such as cancer and heart disease, it has set objectives in terms of health gain but without defining what the contribution of the NHS in meeting those objectives is expected to be.

United Kingdom health spending and the returns-to-investment curve

Given current levels of spending and the relationship between spending and health benefits (the shape of the returns-to-investment curve – *see* Figure 5, p10) where on the curve is the United Kingdom at the moment?

With the government's decision to devote extra resources to the NHS, the answer may seem obvious: where the gradient is steep. However, the Organisation for Economic Co-operation and Development (2004b), for example, has argued that there may be declining returns to further spending, particularly in the short run. Others, taking a long view, have come to the same conclusion: for example, Le Fanu (1999) has argued that the golden age of medicine is over. In his words (p 394), 'by the 1970s, much of what was "do-able" had been done'. This would imply that the flat part of the curve was reached decades ago. Others argue the opposite: recent advances in knowledge imply more is 'do-able' now than ever before (for example, *see* Sikora 2002).

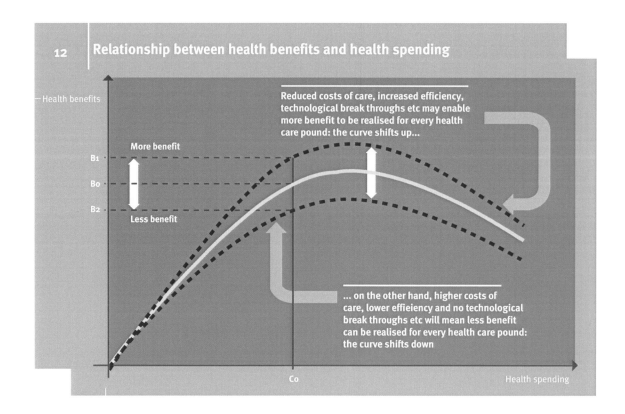

Reduced costs of care, increased efficiency, technological break throughs etc may enable more benefit to be realised for every health care pound: the curve shifts up...

... on the other hand, higher costs of care, lower effieiency and no technological break throughs etc will mean less benefit can be realised for every health care pound: the curve shifts down

Health benefits

More benefit

B1

Bo

B2

Less benefit

Co

Health spending

Figure 12 indicates how the returns to investment can change depending on changes in the costs of providing health care or the efficiency with which care is provided.

There are a number of reasons why the cost of providing a given health care service may rise with time. Some of these are general while others are specific to the NHS.

■ NHS/health care delivery is labour intensive (particularly some parts of hospital care) and offers little scope for capital/labour substitution in response to the increases in real pay levels that can be anticipated as average earnings rise in the economy as a whole.

■ The cost of nursing services is rising at the margin because of the need to recruit more nurses from a limited labour pool. This is only partially offset by overseas recruitment.

■ The supply price of doctors is in part rising for social reasons (that is, an unwillingness by doctors to work unsocial or long hours). The implementation of EU rules on working hours and changes to the GP and consultant contracts mean that working time that was previously largely free to the NHS must now be paid for, without any obvious return in terms of increased effectiveness.

■ Increasing concern about safety and other quality initiatives require greater regulation and other indirect care costs including clinical governance systems within trusts as well as external monitoring and inspection. The Healthcare Commission (2004) has recently taken the lead in reducing the burden of these costs by eliminating duplication and overlaps. But this may succeed only in reducing the rate of increase of these costs rather than their absolute level.

■ Costs to the NHS from compensation claims have risen rapidly in recent years despite attempts to reduce them. The measures being taken to reduce errors and improve quality should work to counteract this trend but the main driver – a society-wide tendency to seek redress from perceived failings in public and other services – seems unlikely to weaken.

TABLE 1 USE OF EXTRA NHS RESOURCES (2004/05–2005/06)	2004/5		2005/6	
	£m	% of previous year's allocation	£m	% of previous year's allocation
Pay and price inflation				
Pay	1085	2.64	1312	2.84
Non-pay	219	0.53	257	0.56
Clinical negligence	183	0.45	58	0.13
Secondary care drugs	190	0.46	199	0.43
Revenue cost of capital	186	0.45	105	0.23
Reform and quality				
Consultant contract	27	0.07	200	0.43
Agenda for change	490	1.19	460	1.00
Working time directive	70	0.17	0	0.00
NICE guidance	304	0.74	328	0.71
Investment in new capital	37	0.09	184	0.40
Technical adjustments				
Pension indexation rebasing	1200	2.92	0	0.00
Revaluation of NHS estate	0	0.00	134	0.29
Total spending commitments	3991	9.72	3237	7.01
Total cash	46162		50469	
Cash increase	5086	12.38	4307	9.33
Change allowing for cost and other spending commitments	1095	2.4	1070	2.2

None of these can be evaluated with any precision, however, the table above provides an indication of their significance. It sets out how the extra resources allocated to the NHS have been used for 2004/05 and 2005/06. It suggests that over half of the allocations to the English hospital and community health services in 2004/05 and 2005/06 has been absorbed in cost increases rather than service expansion or improvement.

At first sight this does not fit with the earlier evidence suggesting that medical advances have been the main cost driver. What seems to have happened is that, for the reasons set out above, there has been a strong relative cost shift due in part to the need to recruit more staff rapidly and to buy out existing medical contracts. In theory these buyouts and the new forms of contracts that have been introduced should lead to greater staff productivity.

However, the evidence so far suggests that only a modest increase in activity has resulted from the extra spending of recent years. As a result, crude productivity measures linking activity to extra staff or extra spending point to a decline (see Figure 13 overleaf). On this

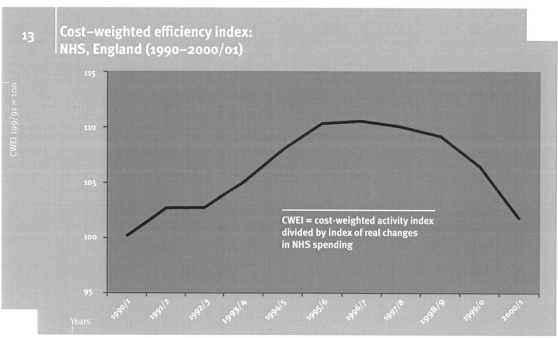

13 Cost–weighted efficiency index: NHS, England (1990–2000/01)

CWEI = cost-weighted activity index divided by index of real changes in NHS spending

Source: Department of Health

basis it would seem that the cost of providing health care is rising and the marginal benefit per unit expenditure is falling – unless the extra costs are being offset by higher benefits.

However, not much weight can be put on this evidence. Many forms of activity are not fully recorded and the 'units of output' (for example, operations) are not constant. The government has therefore ceased to use the index shown in Figure 13. New estimates by the Office of National Statistics using more detailed data show a slightly different picture, although it maintains the general conclusion of falling productivity in recent years (Pritchard 2004). The government is committed to finding an alternative measure that gives a fuller picture of how the NHS is performing as a producer of care in response to the Atkinson inquiry into productivity (Atkinson 2005). However, it has recently set out ideas for tackling this issue and preliminary estimates of the impact on productivity of taking into account aspects of quality such as health gain and patient experience (Department of Health 2005a).

Can greater efficiency offset rising costs?

The evidence of declining productivity may be explained by the effect of the various factors set out above. It may also be explained, as the Organisation for Economic Co-operation and Development (OECD) (2004a) has suggested, by the rapid increase in the NHS budget – too rapid for it to be absorbed efficiently. If this is correct, then the recent decline in productivity might be regarded as a temporary phenomenon, and productivity in the simple terms described in Figure 13 will once again begin to rise.

During the 1980s and 1990s governments assumed that the NHS could increase its efficiency as a producer of care. This was reasserted by the 'fully engaged scenario' set out in the first Wanless report (Wanless 2002) and developed further in the second review (Wanless 2004), which assumed that efficiency could be increased by between 2.5 and 3 per cent a year.

The NHS Plan (Department of Health 2000a) also assumed that efficiency could be improved. Through the establishment of the Modernisation Agency it aimed to spread best practice throughout the NHS in order to achieve increased productivity. In addition, targets were set – for example, for day surgery rates – and other measures were introduced to improve bed utilisation, for example through better discharge arrangements into the community.

Day surgery rates have risen, although not as fast as projected, but length of stay has remained largely unchanged in recent years (historically this would have been a key source of efficiency gains). However, recent studies of US best practice suggest that further savings of this kind are achievable (Feachem *et al* 2002) and that, through better clinical management and better use of IT systems, more widespread gains are possible. It remains unclear, however, whether these savings can be achieved within the NHS since this would depend at least in part on cultural factors, which may be hard to replicate within a very different political and social environment. Nonetheless, the government's modernisation agenda implies that there may be scope for improving productivity through changes in the roles of health care workers, such as allocating prescribing rights to a wider range of professionals or reallocating tasks between different types of staff. Similarly, there is scope for improvement in service delivery through more widespread adoption of new working methods, most of which have already been tested out within the NHS (NHS Modernisation Agency 2004). But evidence of the *scale* of their impact if more widely adopted is not yet available.

Recent OECD (2004b) surveys of health care reform point to a large range of measures, but none are shown to reliably deliver gains sufficient to reduce spending in total, although they may reduce the rate of increase. Many of these measures are already in place in the English NHS, or are in the process of being introduced.

Indeed, in the reformist league, the NHS is a frontrunner rather than a laggard, but its experience suggests that even apparently major reforms (such as GP fundholding) produce only modest efficiency gains, while the impact of some changes such as trust status are not even detectable (Le Grand *et al* 1998).

However, the reform programme now being introduced by the present government already goes far beyond those introduced in the 1990s, so the effects may be more far-reaching over time. The introduction of Payment by Results (PbR) and the (historically) large purchases of diagnostic procedures and operations now beginning to have an impact represent the largest stimulus to NHS efficiency ever introduced. The government may well consider yet further development of the private sector role in direct care to patients, service management and administrative functions. Following the precedent of other service industries, these reforms might even include the use of off-shore locations.

It is too early to estimate what the impact of these new policies may be. But the costs of the contracts so far negotiated with private sector providers involved in independent sector treatment centres (ISTCs), some of which are above NHS cost levels, do not suggest that major gains can be achieved by this route.

Taking the evidence available, it appears that these reforms will not be substantial enough to offset the forces making for higher costs, although it is not possible to prove this. As a result, relative cost shifts will continue to work in an upward direction and thereby shift the returns curve downwards.

Are there increasing benefits of extra NHS spending?

Of course rising spending is, by itself, insufficient evidence that marginal returns are declining. It may also still be that returns are rising – that is, that the whole returns curve is shifting upwards or that extra spending produces extra benefits in terms of access rather than health outcome. Given the government's explicit aim of catching up with other countries, the expectation might be that, during this process, the benefits of extra spending would be particularly high.

As noted above, there are a number of different types of benefits or outcomes that might be associated with extra spending (or, indeed, any particular level of spending) that patients might value. While the primary outcome of a clinical intervention might be some increase in 'healthiness' (from some state of unhealthiness), this might be measured in various ways – increased life expectancy, greater mobility, increased happiness, reduced pain and so on. In addition, there are likely to be benefits that would primarily be classified as unrelated to health, such as convenient booking systems, or benefits connected more with the process rather than outcome of care, such as being treated with respect and dignity. Policy decisions on the use of NHS funds will produce a different mix of all these types of benefits, and the emphasis on certain outcomes rather than others will change over time. Indeed, as the Secretary of State for Health, Patricia Hewitt, has stated (Secretary of State for Health 2005):

> *Patients want to be cared for as individuals, treated with dignity and respect, made to feel welcome, and certainly kept safe. They want to feel as though the NHS cares more about their time and convenience than it does about its own. And they want to understand what's happening to them, to be involved in decisions about their treatment and given a greater say over their care. That's what I mean by a patient-led NHS.*

However, the government has also argued that the NHS has been a poor clinical performer: services have been poorly organised, too little regard has been paid to safety and quality, and the interests of the user have been neglected. Accordingly, it set in train a series of service reforms aimed at improving the design and delivery of care, health outcomes and user experience. In particular these included the introduction of national service frameworks for the main diseases. Other reforms, such as reductions in the working hours of junior doctors, have been designed to improve the working lives of NHS employees.

Figure 14 opposite is a benefits–cost matrix, similar to a programme budgeting approach. The central problem – as in programme budgeting – is attaching a value to the benefits and costs associated with different types of outcomes and different spending/policy areas. As it stands, Figure 14 does not take account of the distribution of benefits. This is not an insignificant failing of the cost–benefit approach, although there are, in principle, ways to accommodate this further benefit dimension. For example, it is possible to use weights on health outcomes such as QALYs to reflect societal preferences regarding the distribution of benefits.

14 | Cost–benefit spending/ policy matrix

Type of benefit	Policy/spending area									Benefit (£)
	Cancer	Heart disease	Mental health	Maximum waiting times	Emergency care	Chronic care	Etc			
Access Waiting time Travel time Booking...										
Process Respect Friendliness Length of stay										
Outcome Lives Life years QALYs... Non-health benefits										
Cost (£)										

A matrix of this kind could have been used to present the expected gains from the NHS Plan and subsequently for each of the national service frameworks. In this way the government could have presented an explicit justification or business case for the extra resources it decided to allocate to the NHS from 2000 onwards. It would also have served as a benchmark against which progress and achievement could have been measured in the years that followed.

In fact, neither the NHS Plan nor the national service frameworks offered a framework of this kind. What follows, therefore, is an attempt to give some indication of the scale and nature of the benefits they are producing based on other reports.

In light of this, what is the hard evidence that health and other benefits have increased as a result of these initiatives (and, of course, extra funding)? This can be examined through three perspectives: the government's three priority disease areas (cancer, heart disease and mental illness), services areas (such as emergency and elective care), and patients' experience of the NHS.

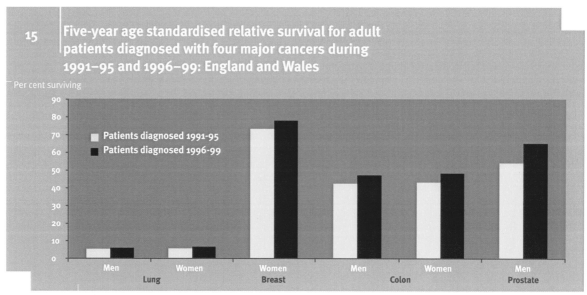

Source: ONS

Benefits for priority diseases
CANCER

The government inherited a commitment to improve cancer services – which in the 1990s had been shown to be fragmented and poorly organised. After a cancer summit involving the Prime Minister and leading clinicians, a national cancer director was appointed in 1999 and, in the following year, *The NHS Cancer Plan* (Department of Health 2000b) was published, which explicitly acknowledged that cancer survival rates in England were lower than in most other European countries. This suggested that there was substantial scope for health gain if services were improved. Subsequently the government allocated substantial sums to implement the proposals set out in the cancer plan.

Reports on the progress of the plan suggest that, in operational terms, performance is getting better (Department of Health 2004a). The two-week maximum waiting target set for initial consultation, introduced in 1998, has resulted in shorter times for those identified as urgent by their GP. In some cases, this has been at the expense of those judged to be non-urgent who do turn out to have cancer.

There is as yet no clear link to survival chances for even the main cancers from the measures set out in the plan. The first review of the plan by the National Audit Office (2004) provided evidence that delays in presenting with the disease appeared to be a significant explanation of England's poor relative performance. However, it was unable to provide evidence of the scale of this effect or of the impact of changes in the organisation of cancer care, such as increasing specialisation among surgeons.

In recent years the death rate from cancer has declined, and the proportion of those treated who survive more than five years after diagnosis has risen. However, these trends were apparent before the plan was implemented; indeed, the latest data available predate its publication (*see* Figure 15). Furthermore, unlike plans in other sectors, the cancer plan

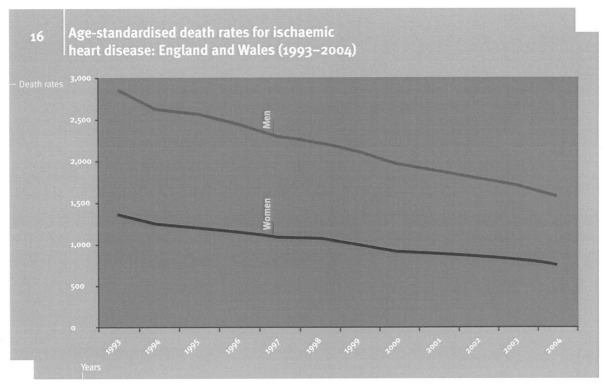

Age-standardised death rates for ischaemic heart disease: England and Wales (1993–2004)

Death rates

Men

Women

Years

Source: ONS

does not define what would happen in the absence of higher spending and the changes in service design and delivery that it is making possible. In other words, it provides no forecast (and the monitoring reports no estimate) of the difference the extra expenditure is making to the cancer burden.

HEART AND CARDIOVASCULAR DISEASE

The *National Service Framework for Coronary Heart Disease* (Department of Health 2000c) set a target for reducing death rates from heart disease by 40 per cent by 2010. A progress report published in 2005 (Department of Health 2005b) claimed that the wider use of statins is saving 9,000 lives a year, although it does not identify the number of QALYs which it believes have been saved. It also pointed to other improvements likely to have a direct effect in saving lives, particularly the rapid application of thrombolytic drugs in accident and emergency departments and reductions in waiting times for surgery. However, it does not acknowledge that waiting times for some procedures have risen.

Given that, in the words of the report, 'seven years ago, cardiac services were in a terrible state' (p 3), the increase in resources made available during this period, and the strong clinically led implementation of higher service standards and service redesign, would be expected to lead to significant health benefits. However, what the report does not show is the impact of the improvements it describes that have already taken place, and those which are planned (in what is described as a ten year programme). So, for example, although overall death rates from ischaemic heart disease fell by 25 per cent between 1997 and 2004, the contribution of health care to that decline (and its future contribution) remains unclear. The progress report does not attempt to identify its past contribution or its future impact.

MENTAL HEALTH

In 1999 the government published the *National Service Framework for Mental Health* (Department of Health 1999) which set out a large number of desirable service improvements, particularly for those provided in the community. But hospital admissions for serious mental illness show few signs of decline.

The only specific health gain target was for a reduction in the rates of suicide and deaths from violent injury. Suicides have indeed fallen but, as with heart disease, this represents a continuation of a long-term trend. The government claims that its policies have ensured the reduction continues, but there is no way of demonstrating this.

Benefits for services

EMERGENCY CARE

In recent years a number of changes designed to reduce waiting times have been introduced to the way that emergency care is provided. These include reductions in the number of departments, more consultant involvement and the widespread introduction of admission or observation wards.

In some areas – such as the rapid administration of anti-thrombolytics – there are certainly health gains. The same is possibly true of improvements in ambulance response times for the small minority of patients for whom very rapid access to hospital is vital to saving their lives.

Accident and emergency departments have also been the focus of successful attempts to reduce waiting times. The four-hour target set in the NHS Plan has been generally achieved, although modified in detail to allow for cases where it does not make clinical sense.

ELECTIVE CARE

The government has made reductions in waiting times for elective care its main target. Delay – and uncertain delay – imposes a wide range of economic and personal/psychological costs, as well as some clinical risks. Despite the complaints of clinicians, the government has been able to ensure that the most urgent cases are dealt with first; that is, the bulk of those waiting for care experience short waits. The number of very long waiters is small and it is these waits that current policies have been successful in reducing. There is evidence (Harrison and New 2000) that long delays lead to increased mortality from some conditions such as heart disease so the substantial reductions achieved for some forms of heart surgery have probably led to health gains.

However, the prospect of further gains from reductions in waiting times is limited by the very success of the government's policies. Unlike other areas of health care, there is a clear limit to what can be achieved. Although complete elimination of all delays is unlikely in the near future, achieving the new 18-week target in England should mean that virtually all the potential health gain from shorter waiting times is achieved, along with reducing the other effects on people's lives arising from uncertainty about when treatment would be available.

As in other policy areas, there is little data on both the direct and opportunity costs of pursuing reductions in maximum waiting times, although over the last five years or so they may have been substantial. There is even less knowledge about the costs as well as the benefits of further reductions – as promised in *The NHS Improvement Plan* (Department of Health 2004b).

CHRONIC CARE

Until recently chronic care had received very little direct attention from policy-makers. With the publication of *The NHS Improvement Plan* (Department of Health 2004b) it now seems set to become a key element in health care policy.

The immediate driving force behind this change has been the perception that poor quality care for those suffering from chronic disease leads to unnecessary hospital admissions. A recent King's Fund report (Dixon *et al* 2004), using evidence from US-managed care organisations, suggested that there is scope for reducing hospital use as well as improving the quality of care received by patients judged at risk of admission through better management of individual patients. These methods are currently being piloted in England. Full results are not yet available but the evidence so far suggests that gains have been limited. Evidence from other countries also indicates that the overall cost reductions may be modest as savings in admissions are offset by the extra costs of the care received by those offered intensive community-based treatment. Improvements in the quality of care are achievable and valued by patients (Segal *et al* 2003, Fireman *et al* 2004). However, there does not appear to be a study which has measured these benefits in ways that would allow a comparison to be made with the benefits which might be achieved by other forms of service improvement.

NHS DIRECT

The rapid introduction of NHS Direct and its establishment as the largest service of its kind in the world represents a major achievement in its own right. It has proved popular, at least in terms of the number of people making use of the service. It is less clear what health benefits NHS Direct has created. A report from the National Audit Office (2002) found that (p 3):

> ... the best estimate that can be generated from available data suggests that NHS Direct is off-setting around half of its running costs by encouraging more appropriate use of NHS services. The gain results from advising a significant number of callers who would otherwise have visited their GPs on how to care for themselves instead. The remaining half of its running costs can be set against the benefits of reassuring callers and saving them unnecessary anxiety.

In other words, it is producing some cost savings but not enough to justify its introduction, no obvious health gain but some, as yet unquantified, gains in terms of user experience and, as the National Audit Office asserts, an unquantified gain in reduced anxiety.

NEW DRUGS

Expenditure on drugs has risen rapidly in the recent past. In part this is due to the wider use of drugs recommended by NICE subsequently becoming generally available within the NHS.

Nearly all the evaluations on which NICE has based its recommendations support the view that the new drugs will produce health gains. These measures, although subject to considerable margins of error because of the limited nature of the evidence available, provide some assurance that the new drugs becoming available to the NHS do provide a reasonable return (although, as noted earlier, the evaluative framework used by NICE is limited to a narrow comparison that sometimes, but not always, involves alternatives to the intervention being assessed).

Two points are worth noting about the interventions so far investigated by NICE. First, it has identified no 'blockbusters': that is, very beneficial drugs for major care groups. The gains are typically modest and experienced by a narrow group of patients. Second, the assessment process provides no guarantee that expenditure on new drugs will provide more benefit than if it was used on other drugs or other services for different diseases. This point is examined in more detail below.

Patient experience

Government statements (for example, *see* Secretary of State for Health 2005) have made it clear that a prime aim of its reforms has been to improve the patient's experience of using the NHS and to improve access to it. There is substantial evidence that they have succeeded in doing so, at least in England.

For example, in the case of cancer, a study by the National Audit Office (2004) reported a number of process improvements including speed of referral, better communication with professionals and better information about patients' conditions.

The Healthcare Commission now regularly monitors patient views at national level. The longest series of such surveys has been carried out by the Picker Institute. Its survey of patient opinion between 1998 and 2004 found that (2005, p 14):

> *Patients' experience has improved significantly in those areas that have been the subject of coordinated action eg hospital waiting times, cancer care and coronary heart disease.*

Overall, the institute came to the view that patients' experience of the NHS in England was improving, but that there was a long way to go before the service could be said to be truly patient-centred.

The improvements reported in surveys such as these provide support for the conclusion that the apparent fall in NHS productivity in recent years has been offset (at least to some extent) by improvements in quality. But there does not appear to be any evidence bearing on the *cost* of achieving these improvements nor, importantly, on the *value* that might be attached to the benefits they produce. This need to improve standard measures of productivity (and output more generally) has been recognised (Atkinson 2005) and a number of approaches have been identified. But so far no effective progress has been made in bringing new measures into use.

Overview

The lack of definitive data in many key areas means that it is impossible to come to a firm conclusion as to where the NHS (in England) is located on the returns-to-investment curve set out in Figure 5 (*see* p 10). Recent reviews of the performance of the NHS have emphasised how few conclusions can be drawn on whether or not particular services have improved (Leatherman and Sutherland 2003; Healthcare Commission 2004; King's Fund 2005).

However, from the limited data that exist the NHS does not appear to be achieving a high health return from the additional spending (that is, it is not on the steepest part of the returns curve). In no area among those reviewed can the major health gains identified be attributed to extra health spending alone. Improvements have been recorded for the priority disease areas, but the contribution of NHS expenditure cannot be isolated from the other factors at work.

Gains are being achieved in areas such as convenience and process benefits (for example, the changes that have led to shorter waiting times within hospital accident and emergency departments). Some of these may lead to better health outcomes, but the main argument used by the government for setting targets such as these derives from the perception that 'expectations' of service performance are rising and that people want choice of when and where to be treated, and easier access to whatever services they choose. While this is convincing intuitively, there is in fact very little hard evidence about the value placed on benefits of these kinds, nor indeed about the costs of providing these benefits. Evidence of *use*, such as that cited in the chief executive's reports to the English NHS (Department of Health 2005c) in respect of walk-in centres and other new facilities, is not evidence of *benefit*.

As has been shown above (*see* Chapter 1), the NHS will soon no longer be able to use the European comparative argument to make a case for more spending. Once the existing spending plans have been fulfilled, the case for more spending will have to be made on the basis of the benefits expected to accrue from it. The next chapter considers what needs to be done if that case is to be made.

In summary:

- recent developments suggest that the costs of providing episodes of health care are rising
- there is only limited evidence of success in countering this trend, so increasingly radical measures are likely to be tried
- there is limited evidence that current spending increases are producing health gains: the main benefits appear to be in the form of improved process and ease of access.

4 Can a limit be set for spending on health?

This paper began with the possibly alarmist suggestion of a future for the United Kingdom where health care spending grew at such a rate as to consume unfeasibly large proportions of the nation's wealth. Historically, health care spending in the United Kingdom has been low by international standards, particularly from the mid-1970s up to the late 1990s (*see* Figure 17 below).

However, what Figure 17 also shows is a generally inexorable upward trend in health care spending as a proportion of GDP across the European Union. A crude time-trend projection of average EU spending shows a continuation of this trend into the future (*see* Figure 18 overleaf). By 2007/08 (the end of the 2004 spending review period), total United Kingdom health care spending is likely to match the lower projected limit for the (weighted) average across the EU.

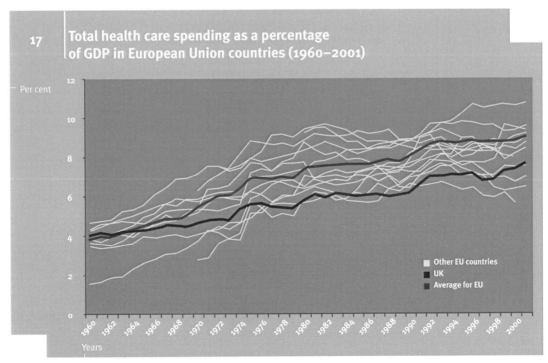

17 **Total health care spending as a percentage of GDP in European Union countries (1960–2001)**

Source: OECD Health data file 2004
Calculations: Authors' own

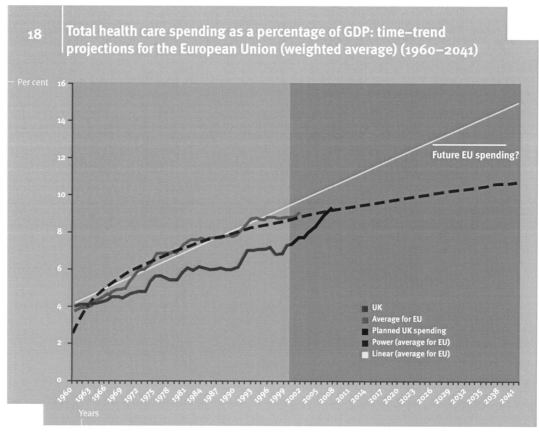

18 Total health care spending as a percentage of GDP: time–trend projections for the European Union (weighted average) (1960–2041)

Source: Authors' own

Is a limit to health spending necessary?

Looked at in this way, perhaps there is less to worry about regarding the future of health care spending in the United Kingdom; after all, spending will have increased to move the United Kingdom from near bottom in the EU spending league to just about the middle of the rankings.

However, a less relaxed – but perhaps more realistic – conclusion to draw is that controlling health care spending is a problem that all industrialised countries face and one that the United Kingdom will, after a long period of relative underfunding, also have to grapple with. It is far from obvious, for example, that the higher levels of spending that other countries have enjoyed for substantial periods of time have brought them to a point that is clearly felt to be 'enough'.

The massive increase in health care spending has taken place without any serious examination of the relationship between the input of resources and the expected outputs/health benefits. The best or only justification for this is depicted in Figure 17 (*see* p 41), which shows the United Kingdom's historical spending trends relative to other industrialised countries. With the low levels of spending relative to other countries, there has been a strong presumption of extra benefit in health or other terms to be gained from increased spending.

However, the (English) NHS is now six years into a nine-year period where annual real terms spending growth has averaged around 7 per cent. Over the next three years the presumption that extra spending will remain worthwhile will become less tenable, and the case for more spending will become harder to make in terms of the health benefits it is likely to produce.

From the perspective of an economic evaluation, increased spending on health care is not, however, inherently bad or undesirable. The full calculation requires information not just about the opportunity costs of the inputs to health care, but the value of the benefits of the outputs.

A large number of factors are increasing the cost of supplying health care and hence reducing the health/cost ratio. Existing policies, followed up by more radical measures, may offset but not fully compensate for such increases.

What remains essentially unknowable, however, is the scale, cost and benefits of new technologies, all of which are inherently uncertain. Hence, no limit can be set for ever. Current indications are that the costs of innovation are rising in general, but that may prove incorrect in particular areas.

The need for better data

The review of evidence in the previous chapter served only to show how poor the information is on which to base any judgement on the health returns resulting from the current large increases in the NHS budget. Evidence from countries that spend more than the United Kingdom suggests the health gains from the higher spending levels projected for the coming three to four years may not be large. However, the narrow range of outcome measures available means that only limited weight can be put on such data.

Increasingly, health care systems are supporting those with chronic conditions; but any improvements that better health care makes to the quality – as opposed to the length of patients' lives – is not measured in *any* health care system. Similarly, other forms of benefit, such as ease of access and 'responsiveness', are not measured except in the crudest way (*see*, for example, World Health Organisation 2000). Others, such as the reassurance and confidence that an effective and responsive emergency care service can be provided, are not measured at all.

Until there is clarity as to what factors should be measured and the appropriate data collected, no clear conclusion can be reached about what the extra spending on the NHS has achieved in recent years, still less what it will achieve in the future. Nevertheless, the analysis presented here has a number of implications for what should be done to help define the point where a limit to spending can be set, that is, where 'enough is enough'.

The politics of health spending

Of course, in one sense limits are already imposed more or less successfully by all health care funders through the setting of budgets or maximum spending limits, and by the imposition of restrictions as to how those funds can be spent. Many countries have attempted, but rarely with success, to reduce spending by such means.

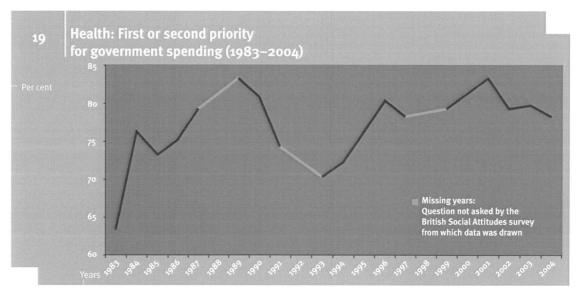

19 | **Health: First or second priority for government spending (1983–2004)**

Source: Appleby and Alvarez: 2005

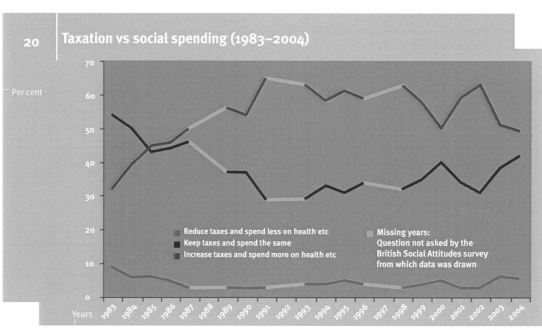

20 | **Taxation vs social spending (1983–2004)**

Source: Appleby and Alvarez: 2005

The budgeting process is, rightly, political. One source of evidence concerning the political decision on spending is the views and attitudes of the public who, apart from being users of the NHS, are also taxpayers and voters. Recent results from the annual British Social Attitudes Survey discussed by Appleby and Alvarez–Rosete (2005) suggest that, despite recent large increases in NHS funding, the public still ranks health as a number one priority for government spending (*see* Figure 19 overleaf). Despite some recent slight reductions, a majority want increases in taxes with extra spending on health care (and other welfare services); very few want taxes and spending reduced (*see* Figure 20 opposite). The voting and taxpaying public's message to politicians would appear to be: don't limit spending (at least not yet).

Voters' views are important, particularly to politicians having to make a decision about NHS spending. However, although the decision involves subjective judgements, this should not imply that such a decision is uninformed by the (objective) facts. As noted earlier, if the public could vote on the size of the NHS budget, the important issue would not be what figure to vote on, but what information they should have to inform their voting.

In light of the discussion so far in this chapter, can a means be found for defining a threshold beyond which spending on health care would not be worthwhile?

For the reasons set out above, such a threshold would be only temporary and subject to adjustment in response to changes in circumstance. Within the economic framework set out in Chapter 2, there is potential for the returns curve to shift downwards if costs rise, or upwards if benefits rise or new sources of benefit are identified.

Therefore the aim is not to define an end point but rather a *means*, when budgets have to be set, of determining whether the returns from more spending are greater than their opportunity costs.

What technical work should inform future spending decisions?

As noted earlier in this paper, the claim has been made that further spending on care is not the best way to improve health. If that claim could be justified then the debate would be radically changed. Therefore, it is worth asking a further question: can the benefits that are derived from spending more on health care services be produced more effectively by other means?

An important overarching issue is the nature of the current policy framework as it bears on the question of spending. The policy framework is characterised by one central fact: no participant, except the Treasury, is faced with an incentive to see health care spending controlled. Because health care is largely free at the point of use, individuals have no financial incentive to moderate their use of services. Nor, generally, do the professionals who provide them, still less the private sector companies that supply drugs and other medical goods. The public is ever more aware of the availability of new treatments, before they are properly trialled, and both the public and professionals are increasingly aware of what other countries spend and provide.

Politicians have the ultimate responsibility for balancing the demands of health care for public funding against other claims on those resources. But they too – most particularly Secretaries of State for Health – have an incentive to stress what health care can achieve rather than the risks and costs entailed in providing it. The government has become an advocate for more spending, promising more and better services. The result is a bias towards spending more, untempered by a scepticism about what the 'more' will achieve in terms of health or any other goals.

With all this in mind, how should the policy framework be adjusted to reduce the pressures to spend more on health?

In Chapter 2 this paper suggested that the most probable shape of the returns-on-investment curve is one where, as spending rises, benefits also rise, but at a decreasing rate, and that there is a point at which the curve flattens out. Somewhere along that stretch of the returns curve a limit has to be set. Benefits at this point will still be positive, but the opportunity costs are steadily rising.

No government has formally set a limit of this kind. However, although its evaluative framework is currently defined very narrowly (and at a level after decisions are made about the overall health budget), there is an obvious analogy between the cost-effectiveness approach of NICE's technical appraisal work and the cost–benefit framework suggested earlier to help inform any decision about a budget limit. NICE's current assessment role not only provides a model for the approach that could be taken to deciding on budget limits, but it could also have a practical role in providing some of the technical information and data that would feed into this decision.

As noted earlier, the decisions made by NICE, in the absence of any government guidelines, do seem to imply a threshold – roughly £35,000–£40,000 per QALY. At the micro-level of the therapy being assessed, this is analogous at the overall budget level of a limit to spending beyond which the returns do not justify the investment. Other factors temper this threshold, with some interventions costing more than £40,000 per QALY being approved and some cheaper interventions being rejected (Devlin and Parkin 2004). Although recommendations from NICE have sometimes been strongly resisted, most recently those in respect of drugs to treat Alzheimer's disease, the notion that there should be some limit to spending based on health gain (measured in QALYs) has come to be widely accepted.

An expanded role for NICE?

If NICE is to provide information critical to overall budget decisions about health then what it assesses, the evidence it needs and how it carries out its assessments will need to change. There are five issues that need to be considered.

First, the current regulatory structure and subsequent arrangements for monitoring the effects of medicines in everyday use cannot be relied on to produce all the evidence which NICE ideally requires to come to its conclusions. Although the regulatory regime for drugs does provide for post-licensing monitoring, it is far from a guarantee that the information required to evaluate their effect is obtained in practice.

Second, and much more important in the long run, NICE is not in a position, unless others have carried out the relevant studies, to make its judgements on the basis of the full potential range of options. In the case of depression, there was enough evidence available for NICE to be able to recommend that drugs should not be the first line of treatment for mild cases. But, in general, the data required for the evaluation of treatment options is not available. This reflects a significant weakness in the current management of publicly funded research and development, and the licensing system. In the current health research economy, the private sector is equipped and motivated to seek new products across only a limited range of the spectrum of possible therapies. Moreover, even though product licensing remains demanding, it is not demanding enough to produce data on comparative performance vis-à-vis existing treatments.

Third, even within its more broadly defined remit which now takes in public health interventions, NICE does not cover the full range of treatments. Nearly all NICE studies concern drugs, and important though these are, they represent only a small part of the total health care budget. This means that many interventions are not properly evaluated: some should be eliminated but others may be more valuable than the new interventions NICE approves (Maynard *et al* 2004). Other interventions may be highly effective if appropriately used but – following Wennberg's argument stated above (*see* p 20) – they may be used beyond this point, yielding modest or even negative returns.

Fourth, NICE evaluations focus on *health* benefits rather than the wider range of benefits that extra health spending may give rise to and which may be valued by patients, such as speed of access.

Finally, some types of intervention fall outside NICE's remit, particularly those which come under the broad rubric of health policy. As set out in the previous chapter, the main focus of much of current health policy is quality of care, better access and other attributes of the way that care is delivered. If it is true that these are becoming increasingly important then the NICE evaluation framework must be radically extended in the ways outlined in the previous chapter.

However, it is currently not NICE's role to evaluate health policy as a whole. That task formally falls to the Department of Health (and informally is taken on by independent researchers and organisations such as the King's Fund). But as the previous chapter made clear, current policy statements and plans are not presented or evaluated holistically (*see* Figure 14, p 33, for an example of a cost–benefit framework). By using the 'catch-up' argument, the government has sidestepped the need to demonstrate what the extra spending on the NHS is producing. However, the data presented in Chapter 2 shows that, once England has 'caught up', spending levels as a proportion of GDP will be no measure of the merits of further spending. Other parts of the United Kingdom have already reached that level, but none has been able to demonstrate what impact its higher budget has had on the health of its residents (or systematically show what other types of benefits have been generated).

To do this, the framework set out in Figure 14 (*see* p 33)could be developed so that the expected benefits and costs of further expansion can be made explicit. The review of the evidence on the link between spending on health care and health (and other forms of benefit) has highlighted what little information exists, as well as demonstrating how difficult it is to reach a full understanding of how the links work.

If the goal of full understanding is too ambitious or prohibitive, then there are ways forward, for example:

- The government has taken the view, supported by focus groups and other survey evidence, that the NHS should be more user-friendly. While the general emphasis of recent policy on non-health benefits may be right, there is a need for quantification of the public's *valuation* of health benefits and associated benefits of health care such as easier and quicker access to care and other aspects of quality. User satisfaction surveys, while helpful, are not enough.
- Systematic use of measures of the health impact of particular procedures should be developed. For example, this could include a before, during and after-care questionnaire for hospital users designed to measure the nature and scale of their health improvement. This would be of particular value in identifying excessive or inappropriate treatment, as well as poor performance of appropriate treatment (Appleby and Devlin 2004).
- Recently, NICE's capacity to carry out evaluations has been reduced. In this proposed expanded role for NICE, there should actually be an extension of the role of the NICE process to areas of treatment where significant resources are involved and where doubts exist about the best forms of treatments, and also to new policy areas where these impact on clinical practice to test whether these produce health gains. Valuation of the benefits of interventions and policies could also fall within NICE's remit and would require evaluation of the best way of eliciting such values.
- The government should take seriously the principles of professional policy-making which it espoused soon after taking office (Strategic Policy Making Team 1999), in particular, more rigorous piloting before 'national rollouts', strengthening internal impact assessments of new policy proposals and extending the use of evaluations.
- For major programmes such as cancer or heart disease, an explicit economic framework for justifying further spending could be used, involving at minimum a baseline forecast of the disease burden in the absence of further spending, comparisons of alternative strategies including traditional forms of intervention, public health measures and changes in personal behaviour.

A programme of work along these lines could be combined with the suggested expanded scope for NICE, the findings of the NHS auditors, the findings of systematic reviews such as those carried out within the Cochrane Collaboration and the results of academic work. This would create a much fuller picture than currently exists of how the NHS is improving the nation's health or creating benefits of other kinds.

Can the benefits of health spending be achieved more effectively in other ways?

The issue here is whether more investment in any or all of the range of measures coming under the public health banner can offer a better return than health care spending. In the past this seems to have been the case: Chapter 2 highlighted the argument – associated with McKeown (1979) in particular – that most improvement in health can be attributed to factors other than the provision of health care.

McKeown's thesis is essentially a historical one. No country has ever planned the balance between treating disease and preventing or reducing it in a systematic way across the full range of services provided by modern health care. If this could be done then more health spending might be effective, but not efficient.

The second Wanless review (Wanless 2004) acknowledged this possibility and therefore examined a so-called 'fully engaged' scenario which sketched out a possible future in which public health policies would reduce the need for health care spending. Its central conclusion is that (p 183):

> After many years of reviews and government policy documents, with little change on the ground, the key challenge now is delivery and implementation, not further discussion. A NHS capable of facilitating a 'fully engaged' population will need to shift its focus from a national sickness services which treats disease, to a national health services which focuses on preventing it.

How is that to be done? Coote (2004) has argued that a basic requirement is a shift in the nature of health care, particularly within community based services (p 25):

> Ideally, what is required is a local health organisation that, as a priority, engages individuals with appropriate knowledge, advice and expertise on how to stay well, offering access to treatment and care as a secondary function.

Coote also argues that such a change can be brought about only if the context in which health care is provided and policy developed is changed. To achieve that will require a fundamental change in the climate of opinion as well as major changes in organisation and policy. While that seems right, it does not follow that the shift Coote proposes would in fact be effective.

Recent government proposals for health trainers fit this model, albeit on a very minor scale. Whether these will be effective or not remains to be seen – the evidence from other similar initiatives is not encouraging. But even if such a 'wellness service' did reduce some demands on health care services such as treatment of minor conditions, it might increase demand on others by making people more aware of the benefits these services might bring.

How should the policy framework be adjusted to reduce the pressures to spend more?

The incentive structure in health is similar to that for other publicly funded services, but from the Treasury's viewpoint is less favourable than, say, for education, since everyone is a potential user and there are well-developed lobbying routes fuelling the pressure to spend more.

Strong commercial, professional and media voices (often fed by researchers) raise awareness of what is medically possible regardless of cost, or of what might theoretically be possible if more was spent on research. Given the financial constraints in the system – the health care budget – the incentive is to ensure that the budget grows. Commercial and professional groups may have little direct voice over this, but they can put pressure on those who decide budgets by using the media to highlight where there are service shortfalls. As Sikora (2002) has so vividly put it (p 567):

> What politician can be seen to condone the refusal a new drug for a young woman with breast cancer pictured with her two beautiful children on the front of a national newspaper?

Within this system of incentives, there is no obvious way of bringing demand and supply into long-term equilibrium. Despite what might now be seen to be very high levels of spending, there is likely to be a perception that enough is still not being spent. The following sections therefore considers the different perspectives of the key stakeholders in the health system and explores whether there is any scope for altering incentives so as to make the concept of a spending threshold more tenable in practice.

Individuals

The demand for health care is influenced by a large number of factors: geography, knowledge and, perhaps most important, individuals' expectations of the value of seeking care. Patients' demands are rarely, if ever, influenced by the cost of care. Of course, from the patient's point of view, the demand for health *care* is derived from a demand for *health*; in reality, it is a professional – a doctor, a nurse – who generally exercises the actual demand for health care, based on their professional knowledge and judgement. The role of the supply-side (the NHS and its staff) in influencing demand and spending is discussed below. However, despite the derived nature of demand for health care, individuals still have to present for potential treatment in the first instance, and, once they have entered the system, their influence on the demand for health care can in turn be influenced, depending on the incentives they face.

So, for example, imposing charges or co-payments on patients for the use of services would, to an extent at least, make the link between consumption and cost real for individuals and hence, at the margin, reduce or limit demand. But the basic principle underpinning the NHS – that services should be free at the point of use – rules out the widespread use of charges to limit demand. Other publicly funded systems make more use of charges than the countries of the United Kingdom, but all protect their citizens from meeting the full costs of provision, even of relatively cheap services such as GP consultations or commonly used drugs.

Worldwide evidence suggests that while charges do deter use of health services, they are not effective in distinguishing between appropriate and inappropriate use. Nevertheless, in the United States, failure of earlier attempts to control the costs of medical insurance has led to proposals for new types of health plans which would require users to pay the first US$1,500 of any claim (Mango and Riefburg 2005).

Two recent policy initiatives in England have a bearing on the incentives faced by individuals: choice and access.

PATIENT CHOICE
Policy on formalising and extending patient choice in the NHS is currently narrowly focused on choice of hospital for outpatient/elective care (although there are plans to extend it to other areas of care). The government's expectation is that offering choice of place of treatment will help to drive down costs and hence raise efficiency in the production of elective care.

However, choice may lead to higher spending in two main ways. First, the direct link created between what a hospital (and sometimes an individual surgeon) does and the income it obtains runs the risk, in the absence of strong purchasing, of over-treatment such as that identified by Wennberg (2004). Given the apparent need to increase the volume of elective care, that risk may currently seem small, but as activity grows and if waiting times fall in line with government targets, it will need to be addressed.

Second, it is easy to see how, even within its currently conceived narrow focus (but within a system where those making the choices do not directly bear the costs of doing so), the government could act to increase expectations of what the NHS can or should deliver and add to spending pressures.

Further, if the domain of choice were to be further expanded – for example, into choice of type of treatment – there should be no expectation that patients will exercise their choice with any reference whatsoever to the criteria of cost or even clinical effectiveness. To counter this risk requires a greater explicitness about the limits to choice, for example, only making available treatments that have been approved by NICE.

'CHOOSING HEALTH' AND ACCESS TO HEALTH CARE

Arising in part from the second Wanless report, the white paper *Choosing Health* (Department of Health 2004c) aims to put fresh impetus behind public health policy. Its main emphasis is on the role of the individual in 'choosing health' (as opposed, presumably, from 'choosing illness' and hence consuming health care that could otherwise be avoided). There is a strong case for emphasising what individuals can do for themselves and what the government and the NHS should do to support them.

But while the thrust of *Choosing Health* is about staying healthy and staying out of the health care system, another set of policies – initiatives to reduce waiting times, NHS Direct, walk-in centres and so on – have been designed to do just the opposite: to encourage easier access to health care services.

Some initiatives – NHS Direct, for example – were in large part designed to relieve demands on other parts of the NHS, for example, general practice and accident and emergency, but the evidence suggests that its impact has been small (Munro *et al* 2005). Instead, it appears to be meeting previously unmet (often relatively low-level) health care needs. Other actions to improve access – for example, to reduce waiting times – have been wholly and deliberately expansionary, with the benefits generally seen, *a priori*, to be worth the costs. However, there is no evidence of the opportunity costs of reductions achieved so far, nor is it completely clear how reductions have been achieved (Harrison and Appleby 2005).

The government's failure to define the *value* to be attached to improvements in access seems to rely on an implicit assumption that access can be expanded in a controlled and limited 'catch up' way. In this view there are few knock-on consequences in terms of increased (rather than easing) pressures on spending through, for example, encouraging greater public and patient expectations or pressures to expand the boundaries of the NHS to address currently unmet needs. But the evidence available (National Audit Office 2004) suggests otherwise.

INFORMATION

In the absence of charges or other effective incentives, the main potential influence on behaviour is information. The government has already accepted the need to provide users with better information about how to improve and promote their own health and has reduced some of the regulatory barriers to their doing so (for example, by expanding the scope for self-treatment through expanding the number of over-the-counter drugs and increasing provision of structured self-care programmes). It has also proposed a series of measures to support healthier lifestyles (Department of Health 2004c).

There is some evidence that such measures may reduce calls on the NHS (Department of Health 2001). But information is a double-edged sword: its wider availability may encourage, as well as discourage, seeking professional help. For example, wider knowledge of risk factors may lead to people being more concerned about their health, and greater knowledge of treatment options may lead to greater use of services rather than less.

The Department of Health has recently established a unit to collate and interpret all the evidence which is being collected on users' experiences of the NHS, good as well as bad. This is an excellent initiative, but it should be extended to include original research into the factors affecting the demand for different NHS services, the links between them, and the realistic potential for managing demand downwards to lower cost forms of provision or to self-care.

Health care providers

As noted above, the government is in the process of introducing patient choice to place of treatment. At the same time, to create the capacity for this, it has encouraged new, non-NHS suppliers to enter what is effectively a new market for health care. How will this new economic environment develop and, through the new incentives it brings, what impact could it have on overall spending?

In two speeches in 2001, the Prime Minister suggested a new view of the role of public services, and the NHS in particular. In the first (Blair 2001a) he said:

> *... so we may be traditional in our view of the best way of financing the NHS; through taxation. But let no one doubt our radicalism on how we wish to provide NHS care. There must be a decisive break with the way the NHS has worked in the past. I see the NHS as founded on a set of values and not a set of rigid structures.*

In the second (Blair 2001b) he argued that:

> *... the point, very simply, is this: the user comes first; if the service they are offered is failing, they should be able to change provider; and if partnership with other sectors can improve a service, the public sector should be able to do it.*

These two extracts typify the government's policy on public services: that equity in financing health care is best achieved through mildly progressive general taxation, but that the patient/consumer should be sovereign through the exercise of choice of health care provider – whether public or private – with providers reimbursed by taxpayers' health care contributions on the basis of actual work done. In other words, *ownership* of the means of health care production is not a defining characteristic of health care (in England at least), and choice coupled with stronger financial incentives provides the levers to better align what providers offer with what patients want.

How far this policy will extend remains unclear. It could eventually lead to a mix of patients, GPs and state purchasers of one form or another contracting with and buying care from a wholly independent set of private, voluntary and quasi-public/private providers.

What such a changed economic environment will mean for health care spending is not easy to foresee. At one level, the historic control of NHS expenditure through the traditional political process would remain. However, as has already been noted in relation to patient choice, pressures on spending are likely to be increased rather than reduced. The creation of a degree of competition between providers, together with the new reimbursement system PbR, may or may not exert downward pressure on production costs and crudely increase taxpayers' 'bang per buck'. Similarly, the existence of a greater plurality of health care providers may simply create yet another pressure group for more spending.

The incentive structures now being put in place through the establishment of foundation trusts and the introduction of PbR may be effective in encouraging the NHS to deliver more elective care more cheaply. There is a risk, however, that it will reward the strongest players in the system – the acute hospitals – for carrying out more activity where it is not necessary, for example, where alternatives are more effective, or where the procedures are of low value.

Where elective care is concerned, to counter this risk requires agreement on clinical thresholds to define when intervention is appropriate and worthwhile. In respect of emergency care, the main need is to ensure that appropriate alternatives to admission exist and that users are guided to them.

Where incentives go, the next step is to reward providers for lower levels of activity in the way that some regulated power utilities are rewarded for energy conservation measures. That will be very hard to achieve within the financial framework currently being created which rewards greater activity, including higher levels of emergency admissions, even though the government has set a target for reducing the number of emergency admission days.

How the incentives embodied in PbR to increase 'profitable' activity – that is, where marginal costs are less than the national tariff – will work out in the aggregate is difficult to predict; linking payment to activity may not automatically increase activity overall. In addition, there is a countervailing force in the system – purchasers (PCTs) – whose government-derived objectives (to, for example, manage secondary care demand) could limit pressures for more spending. The strength of this force, however, depends on the effectiveness of commissioning by PCTs.

The pressure for more admissions reflects a number of factors, including long-term social changes (Kendrick 1996), which the NHS can do little about. But it may also reflect changes in clinical thresholds both for referral and admission as well as continuing failures within the community in respect of people with chronic conditions. Until these factors are better understood, the appropriate policy response in terms of new incentives or other measures is unclear.

On balance, the mix of policies and associated rhetoric that has emerged since publication of the NHS Plan has not helped to promote a climate of opinion which recognises that a line has to be drawn somewhere. The government would argue that it has had to emphasise the need to improve services and access to them in order to ensure that its overriding objectives of ensuring free and equal access for equal need are met. There is force in that argument; the irony is that the more it improves services and access the harder these objectives are to attain in the long run.

Treasury

It is clear that the Treasury's preferred spending path is the Wanless (2002) 'fully engaged' scenario, which is not only the least costly but also holds out the prospect, according to Wanless, of spending settling down to a constant proportion of GDP by 2017/18 at around 10.6 per cent of UK GDP.

In effect, then, the Treasury has set a limit to NHS spending and has relied on the 2002 Wanless review to justify this. However, as was noted in Chapter 1, the justification given in the Wanless review for this scenario appears to rest primarily on the notion of 'catching up' and then 'keeping up' with spending in other (mostly) European countries. However, there must be considerable doubt – even if the population does become 'fully engaged' – that this limit is tenable on these terms; the experience of countries already spending near or at this proportion of GDP on their health care (such as Canada, France and Germany) is not one of unmitigated satisfaction on the part of patients, the public and policy-makers. To this extent, NHS funding policy fails to address the question of when 'enough is enough'. This does not mean that 'enough' has been spent when everyone *is* completely satisfied. Rather, in the absence of the cost–benefit approach argued for in this paper (and the implicit need to generate the right information to inform that approach), simply aiming to catch up and keep up would do little to either improve satisfaction or necessarily coincide with a more efficient allocation of society's scarce resources.

The Treasury has of course been implicitly answering the question of what is enough for decades as part of its role as controller of public spending, and in that role it has been highly successful. But that experience has not equipped it to answer (or even to pose) the questions that now need to be answered about the benefits which health spending is producing.

At present, relations between the Treasury and the Department of Health (in England) are formalised through a set of public service agreements covering, broadly, goals concerning improvements in health, health care and value for money improvements. However, the Treasury should begin to ask for evidence of a quite different sort, which currently the Department would find hard to provide, on the benefits and costs of the major programmes it is supporting.

The matrix set out in Chapter 3 (*see* Figure 14, p 33) provides a simple template for this. To use it effectively will require results from the work programme set out above into the benefits of extra spending. But a useful first step would be for it to require the department to set out some of its main spending programmes (such as cancer and mental health) within the matrix framework and apply to it the kind of questions that might be applied to any major investment using public funds: What would happen in the absence of more spending? Is the policy mix right? What are new technologies contributing? Where can costs be saved? What are the costs and benefits, at the margin, of reducing waiting times?

Regulators

The importance of new technology as a source of rising expenditure has already been demonstrated. As Mark Pauly (2003) has observed in the context of growing US health care spending (p 3), 'It's technology, stupid'. Pauly also raises the basic economic question concerning the worth of increased health care spending: 'Was the benefit (even if positive) worth the cost?' This question is central to the task of NICE – an organisation with no parallel in the United States.

As has been noted above, NICE is currently the main way in which the NHS (implicitly) defines the line where spending on individual therapies is 'enough'.

This paper has already identified a role for NICE in generating vital evidence through a developed technology and policy appraisal framework to inform the cost–benefit approach to limiting budget decisions. Others (for example, Maynard *et al* 2004) have also suggested that in order to tackle the essential rationing and prioritising task implicit in setting budget limits, the NHS could be barred from adopting technologies until it receives approval from NICE. Maynard and colleagues go further and suggest that NICE should confront the issue of the affordability of its recommendations by working to a real annual budget, making allocations from this budget to NHS organisations based on its technology assessments. In this way, NICE and the NHS would be forced to 'determine the value of the additional therapies at the margin, examine the effect of their decisions on the whole NHS, and also provide incentives to balance cost enhancing and cost reducing recommendations' (Maynard *et al* 2004, p 229).

Measures such as these are, however, essentially tactical. While some of the pressures for greater spending do come from inside the NHS, the pressures from outside – largely the private sector and the wider research community – are at least as strong.

Pharmaceutical industry

For the foreseeable future the NHS and other health care systems will continue to rely on the pharmaceutical and biotechnology industries for new medicines. They have, though, been criticised, most recently by the Health Select Committee, for using undue influence to promote their products (House of Commons Health Committee 2005). The pharmaceutical industry has already accepted, particularly in the United Kingdom, that some of the promotional methods used in the past to influence professionals in particular must be stopped or reduced in scale and that the ban on advertising prescription drugs directly to consumers must be retained (Association of the British Pharmaceutical Industry 2005).

More positively, the government should develop ways of working with the industry that reward health creation where this is not profitable under existing commercial arrangements. The industry, for example, has recognised that public–private partnerships should be used to develop otherwise unprofitable drugs for developing countries (Garnier 2005). The same approach could be used more widely to fill those gaps which are not commercially viable to fill. In principle there are many ways of doing this (Harrison 2003): some will involve major commitments of public funds to encourage developments in neglected areas (Scottish Executive 2005); others may involve altering the incentives facing companies after drugs come to the market, for example, reward schemes that focus on incremental benefits over existing treatments, which are payable only if treatments are successful (Moldrup 2005). The potential impact on NHS spending of such measures is equivocal: pressures to spend more may or may not increase. However, a greater focus on *health* (as opposed to wealth) creation would be more likely to improve the health returns (that is, the benefits) on the NHS pharmaceutical budget.

Department of Health

The prerequisite of this approach is for government to take its own view of where innovation is most desirable. A first step in this direction is for the Department of Health to clarify its own incentives by divesting itself of its role as industry sponsor. As the Health Select Committee put it (House of Commons Health Committee 2005, para 335):

> ... *the interests of patients, the NHS and industry can be at odds and we have no confidence that the Department is capable of achieving the balance required.*

Accordingly it recommended that 'responsibility for representing the interests of the pharmaceutical industry should move into the remit of the Department of Trade and Industry to enable the Department of Health to concentrate solely on medicines regulation and the promotion of health' (para 392). In its response to the Committee, the Department of Health (2005d) indicated that it wanted to maintain its own role, but that it would (p 24) 'put in place formal arrangements to ensure closer cooperation between both Departments...'.

In its role as promoter of the health interest, the Department must begin to shift its thinking from activity to outcomes and benefits, and strengthen its knowledge base in the areas that this paper's analysis has shown to be weak. In doing so it might consider establishing, or funding, the kind of in-house audit that the World Bank conducts on its own activities, one that is genuinely independent and securely funded (World Bank 2005).

It should also reconsider the focus of the research it funds or for which it provides facilities. The bulk of medical research is carried out or paid for by the pharmaceutical industry, but the public sector, including the NHS, is still responsible for more than £1 billion a year. Much of this research is devoted to fundamental science of a kind that, because of its speculative nature, is appropriate for public funding.

The funding made available by the Department of Health has a less clear rationale. A principled research effort would focus on reducing the cost and increasing the effectiveness of current interventions rather than on new and expensive procedures. This would need an organised process for identifying areas of clinical uncertainty (Chalmers *et al* 2005) where trials are required to improve clinical decision-making and that would, among other things, aim to identify the incremental benefits of more expensive treatments. Such a process should give greater weight to the interests of patients, which are often different from those of professionals and researchers, and who would prefer less intensive and less risky forms of intervention than they are offered by current medical technology (Wennberg 2004).

It would also mean examining the scope for alternative treatments – including prevention – in all major cost areas or where costs are rising rapidly. In the case of statins, for example, there are established means of achieving similar benefits through behavioural change (Jenkins *et al* 2003).

Lastly, the review of the evidence in this paper relating to the current contribution of the NHS to health and other objectives has revealed just how little is known. As Wennberg (2004) has complained (p 964): 'The lack of priority given to the evaluative health science is depressing, given the growing evidence that, for populations, greater frequency of use does not improve health outcomes.' Unless this bias is corrected the debate on the limits to spending will not move forward.

The Department has recently published a consultation paper on its research programme. This makes no mention of the issues discussed here; instead, it puts the main emphasis on improving the organisation and management of clinical trials. Spending on programmes such as Health Technology Assessment, which bear on the issues discussed in this paper, remains tiny in comparison to the sums absorbed in the development of new treatments.

The vast majority of private and publicly funded research and development is not devoted to cost control or the promotion of system objectives such as equity of access, but rather increases in the sales of drugs and other devices or new forms of treatment. Given the prevailing pattern of incentives bearing on the health research economy, this is unlikely to change.

Overview

If the argument that a limit to spending on health care should be set is accepted – even, perhaps, a flexible limit responsive to changing technology, societal valuations and so on – then how is it to be set? At one level the answer is straightforward: a limit is set as part of a political process culminating in announcements by the Chancellor in budgets and spending reviews.

However, this political process needs to be informed. While the assessment work of NICE goes some way to addressing the technical issues involved in producing the information on which a judgement about limits could be based, from the point of view of decisions about an overall budget limit, NICE's evaluative approach is imperfect.

Other technical tasks include the measurement on a more systematic basis of the actual health outcomes arising from health care activities and the valuation of benefits of major care programmes within an overall cost–benefit framework.

However, setting limits to spending is not just a technical matter. Within the current policy framework, key actors in the health care system and those with an interest in its spending power operate within a system of incentives that, from the point of view of health care spending, tend to add to pressures to increase spending. Such pressures can be alleviated, but this depends on changing or limiting the scope of some policies, for example patient choice.

Taking a broader view of setting limits, there is scope for achieving some of the benefits generated by health care by other means, in particular through activities more generally thought of as public health interventions (although not exclusively so).

To achieve this, however, would require a major reorientation in the way that health policy is developed. In other words, if there is an effective debate about what constitutes 'enough' within a largely publicly funded health care system, that debate might focus, as it has in some countries, on what should or should not be within the publicly funded health care package.

As this paper has attempted to show, such a debate would need to open up deep issues. Any attempt to define a sustainable medicine runs counter to 'the notion that all progress is affordable, that all progress brings benefit and increased equality of outcome, and that there is a moral duty to pursue progress' (Callahan 1999, p 252). It is these deep-seated notions that must be challenged before an effective debate can begin.

In summary:

■ there is a long way to go before a 'good enough' threshold can be identified across the whole range of health policies and the full range of benefits they produce
■ the current policy framework in general does not support such a threshold: it is encouraging greater use and provision of services
■ there is scope for redirecting innovation but to do so will involve a radical shift in current policies and a new role for the Department of Health
■ there may be scope for reducing the scale of health care needs through measures to promote health and the development of new forms of service, but that remains to be demonstrated in practice.

5 Recommendations

The central theme of this paper has been the need to develop a rational, acceptable and evidence-informed process for arriving at sensible limits to health care spending without abandoning the two core equity values of the NHS: that it is funded in a progressive way (the rich contribute a higher fraction of their income than the poor) and that it is accessible at time of need regardless of non-health factors such as income, geography and so on. Over the last few years the NHS across the United Kingdom, and particularly in England, has enjoyed large increases in funding – in line with public views about the need (and desire) for higher spending. But there is an obvious limit to increases that outstrip the growth of the economy. With the deferment of the 2006 spending review and the decision to engage in a comprehensive spending review in 2007, there is an opportunity to think more deeply about the issues raised in this paper and to begin to formulate appropriate actions and policy.

Future policy choices concerning NHS spending are straightforward to list:

- carry on increasing spending at current rates – that is, postpone the inevitable decision to contain spending
- carry on increased spending at current rates and improve efficiency and productivity – that is, buy extra time before confronting the inevitable decision to contain spending
- align NHS spending growth to general, long-term growth in the economy as a whole with possible adjustments for a modest propensity to devote a greater share of GDP to health care as GDP grows.

The first of these options is likely to be untenable in the medium to long run. The implied health budget would itself be hard to finance, but other programmes – including social care and pensions – are also likely to impose increased demands on the public purse. While this paper's analysis suggests that demographic changes are of only modest importance for health spending, their impact on these two areas of spending is likely to grow and both will be hard to shift to the private sector beyond the share it now accounts for.

The second represents the current position, but this is likely to be viable only for the current planning period – up to 2008.

There are benefits to be gained from pursuit of this option but these gains are unlikely to prove substantial enough to do more than postpone the need to face up to the underlying problem by more than a year or so. They may not even be sufficient to counter the factors making for higher unit costs.

The last of these options must be the medium to long-term goal. It is not an easy option to pursue. If the forces driving up demand and costs cannot be contained, and resistance to increased taxation reaches a critical point, then this option will also bring into sharp relief the need to be explicit about what degree of inequality in health care society is prepared to put up with.

In other words, if the ability of the public health care system to meet increasing demand is constrained by the taxation it can command then, inevitably, the price to be paid will be a growing gap between rich and poor in terms of access to health care and, as a consequence, health status. The well-off, of course, will be more able financially to satisfy their health care demands in private markets.

In the short term the government has forestalled that argument by financing a massive increase in NHS spending and thereby almost silencing those who argue that a publicly financed system will never be able to afford a 'good enough' standard of service. This argument will reappear more strongly once spending growth slows. Of course, the main argument *against* switching away from progressive taxation as a funding source will also be raised: that is, that the trade-off implied by any system that is less progressive will be reductions in fairness in funding; in short, the poor will pay more and the rich will pay less than they do now.

The question now is: can measures be taken that will provide better evidence that the NHS uses its resources wisely and takes on new spending commitments only when they are justified?

The current rate of increase in health spending, at just over 7 per cent above the real rate of GDP growth per annum, is unsustainable. This rate implies a doubling in *real* spending in 11 years and an eight-fold increase in 30 years. Notwithstanding the hypothetical example of expanding NHS spending outlined in Annexe 1, the pressure on the public purse would be immense.

The former Secretary of State John Reid acknowledged this shortly before the end of his time in office (Health Service Journal 2005). But neither he nor his successor Patricia Hewitt has shown any understanding of the implications. In response to the claims that current funding is insufficient to allow the NHS to meet current targets, Hewitt has responded by urging it to improve productivity. That may be feasible; but as long as policies continue to be based on the expansion of facilities and the promotion of demand, more will never be enough. The political rhetoric must change.

However, it cannot do so in a vacuum. If the government were to adopt the economic framework set out in this paper, it would not be able to use the framework effectively because, with the exception of the areas reviewed by NICE, there is little evidence of where the United Kingdom is placed on the returns-to-investment curve – whether this is measured in terms of better health or the broader spectrum of benefits set out in Figure 14 (*see* p 33).

The recommendations therefore fall into two groups: strengthening the knowledge base and changing the policy framework.

Strengthening the knowledge base

How much public money should be spent on the provision of health care is ultimately a political matter. But if such decisions are to be informed by evidence of their implications, then the evidence base bearing on the benefits of additional spending will have to be strengthened. This should include:

- a programme of micro-studies of the benefits of new policy initiatives
- quantification of the public's *valuation* of health benefits and associated benefits of health care
- systematic use of measures of the health impact of particular procedures
- an extension of the role of the NICE process to new areas of treatment and also to new policy areas
- strengthening internal impact assessments and extending the use of evaluations.

Changing the policy framework

This paper has argued that, given the incentives facing individuals, clinical and research professionals and the private sector, more will never be enough. As long as health care is free or nearly so at the point of delivery that will be so, and this will hold true whether or not health care is funded from taxation or social insurance. But there is scope for modifying the current pattern of incentives so as to moderate their impact.

The Department of Health should therefore:

- ensure that the technical agenda set out in the recommendations for strengthening the knowledge base is actively pursued within the benefits–cost matrix devised in this paper (*see* Figure 14, p 33)
- adopt the Health Select Committee's recommendation that the Department should give up its sponsorship role for the pharmaceutical industry
- ensure that the system of financial and other incentives imposed on the NHS, including its users, does not encourage inappropriate treatment but does encourage appropriate reductions in activity
- strengthen the role of NICE and ensure that the publicly funded research programme supports this strengthened role by providing the evidence needed for comparative evaluation of treatment options.

Annexe 1 Sustainable funding

Sustainable funding is often not defined, but may presumably refer to assumptions about increased demand, the possible need for higher taxation and the possibility that a point will be reached when taxpayers will baulk at further increases. In other words, *publicly funded* health care could become 'unaffordable' and hence 'unsustainable'. However, such arguments often fail to take account of the possibilities for expanding spending on health care – even as a proportion of GDP – without the need for sacrificing other forms of private and public spending as long as an economy grows in real terms.

Hence the issue to be tackled is not so much one of sustainability of funding, but the value of the benefits of spending on health care whatever the level of funding.

CAN WE AFFORD TO SPEND 30 PER CENT OF GDP ON THE NHS?

Since 1949/50, the UK economy has grown around three-fold in real terms, UK NHS spending has increased by around seven-fold, and the NHS share of GDP has more than doubled (to around 7 per cent) in 2004/5. This has been achieved while simultaneously increasing real spending on all non-NHS goods and services by nearly three-fold.

But could the UK economy support even higher NHS spending, say 30 per cent of GDP, in the next 50 years? The answer, perhaps surprisingly, is almost certainly yes. If it is assumed that the economy grows at 2 per cent a year (less than historic trends), and NHS spending increases at 5 per cent, by 2055 the economy will have increased by around 170 per cent, NHS spending will have gone up more than ten-fold, and the proportion of the total national wealth spent on the NHS will have increased to around 30 per cent.

This means that spending on all other non-NHS goods and services, both public and private, will have reduced from 97 per cent of GDP to 70 per cent over 50 years. However, as the economy has grown, real spending on all non-NHS goods and services will have *doubled* – despite their share of GDP falling by 27 percentage points.

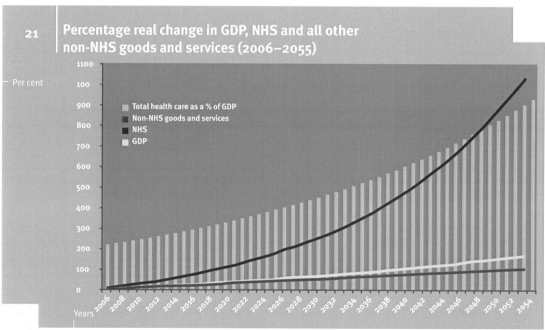

Source: Appleby and Alvarez: 2005

Further, given that income elasticities for some goods and services is less than 1 (for example, food, household goods and so on), spending on these will not increase as fast as the growth in national income, and may even fall for some ('inferior') goods and services. This would leave room for even greater growth in NHS spending without significant sacrifice.

Of course, other goods and services have, like health care, income elasticities greater than 1 (for example, leisure services), implying a growth in spending on such 'luxuries' that would be higher than the growth rate of the economy. It is an empirical matter whether, following the hypothetical example above, the doubling in real spending would be enough to meet the desired increased consumption levels higher national income would imply.

Nevertheless, this hypothetical example suggests that sustainability or affordability arguments against higher shares of national wealth devoted to health care are by no means clear-cut.

Bibliography

Aaron HJ (2003). 'Should public policy seek to control the growth of health care spending?' *Health Affairs*, January web exclusive, W3–28.

Achenbach JP (2000). '*How important have medical advances been?*' in *Improving Population Health in Industrialised Countries*, Sussex J ed. London: Office of Health Economics.

Achenbach JP (1996). 'The contribution of medical care to mortality decline: McKeon revisited'. *Journal of Clinical Epidemiology*, vol 49, pp 1207–13.

Albert X, Bayo A, Alfonso JL, Cortina P, Corella D (1996). 'The effectiveness of health systems in influencing avoidable mortality: a study in Valencia, Spain, 1975–90'. *Journal of Epidemiology and Community Health*, vol 50, pp 320–25.

Appleby J, Alvarez-Rosete A (2005). 'Public responses to NHS reform' in *British Social Attitudes (22nd Report)*, Park A ed. London: Sage.

Appleby J, Boyle S (2000). 'Blair's billions: where will he find the money?'. *British Medical Journal*, vol 320, pp 865–67.

Appleby J, Boyle S, Devlin N, Harley M, Harrison A, Thorlby R (2004a). *What is the Impact of Waiting Times Targets on Clinical Treatment Priorities? Second stage report to the Department of Health*. London: King's Fund.

Appleby J, Devlin N (2004). *Measuring Success in the NHS: Using patient-assessed health outcomes to manage the performance of health care providers*. London: Dr Foster Ethics Committee.

Appleby J, Devlin N, Dawson D (2004). *How Much Should We Spend on the NHS? Issues and challenges arising from the Wanless review of future health care spending*. London: Office of Health Economics, King's Fund and University of York, Centre for Health Economics.

Association of the British Pharmaceutical Industry (2005). *Code of Practice for the Pharmaceutical Industry*. London: ABPI.

Atella V, Marini G (2002). 'Is health care expenditure really a luxury good? A reassessment and new evidence based on OECD data'. Social Science Research Network web page, http://ssrn.com/abstract=383004

Atkinson AB (2005). *Atkinson Review: Final report measurement of government output and productivity for the national accounts*. Basingstoke: Palgrave Macmillan.

Aylin P, Tanna S, Bottle A, Jarman B (2004). 'Dr Foster's case notes: How often are adverse events reported in English hospital statistics?'. *British Medical Journal*, vol 329, p 369.

Baum M (2004). 'Does the act of surgery provoke activation of "latent" metastases in early breast cancer'. *Breast Cancer Research*, vol 6 (4), pp 160–61.

Blair A (2001a). *The Prime Minister's speech on public service reform.* 16 October, www.number-10.gov.uk/output/Page1632.asp

Blair A (2001b). *The Prime Minister's speech on the NHS.* 6 December, www.number-10.gov.uk/output/Page1674.asp

Bonaccorso SN, Surchio JI (2002). 'Direct to consumer advertising is medicalising normal human experience: against'. *British Medical Journal*, vol 324, p 910.

Buck D, Eastwood A, Smith PC (1999). 'Can we measure the social importance of health care?'. *International Journal of Technology Assessment in Health Care*, vol 15, pp 89–107.

Bullock H, Mountford J, Stanley R (2001). *Better Policy Making.* London: Centre for Management and Policy Studies, Cabinet Office.

Bunker JP (2001). *Medicine Matters After All: Measuring the benefits of medical care, a healthy lifestyle, and a just social environment.* London: The Nuffield Trust.

Callahan D (2003). *What Price Better Health? Hazards of the research imperative.* Berkeley, CA: University of California Press.

Callahan D (1999). *False Hopes: Overcoming the obstacles to a sustainable, affordable medicine.* New Brunswick, NJ: Rutgers University Press.

Canadian Health Services Research Foundation (2003). *Myth: The cost of dying is an increasing strain on the healthcare system.* Ottawa: CHSRF.

Chalmers R, Jobling R, Chalmers I (2005). 'Is the NHS willing to help clinicians and patients reduce uncertainties about the effects of treatments?'. *Clinical Medicine*, vol 5 (3), pp 230–34.

Commission for Health Improvement (2004). *Unpacking the Patients' Perspective: Variations in NHS patient experience in England.* London: Commission for Health Improvement.

Coote A (2004). *Prevention Rather than Cure.* London: King's Fund.

Cutler DM (1995). *Technology, Health Costs, and the NIH.* Harvard University and the National Bureau of Economic Research. Paper prepared for the National Institutes of Health Economics Roundtable on Biomedical Research, Cambridge, MA.

Cutler D, Kadiyala S (1999). *The Economics of Better Health: The case of cardiovascular disease.* Mimeo, Harvard University.

Cutler DM, McClellan M (2001). 'Is technological change in medicine worth it?'. *Health Affairs,* vol 20 (5), pp 11–29.

Cutler D, McClellan M, Newhouse JP (1999). 'The costs and benefits of intensive treatment for cardiovascular disease' in *Measuring the Prices of Medical Treatments,* Triplett J ed. Washington, DC: Brookings Institution Press.

Department of Health (2005a). *Healthcare Output and Productivity: Accounting for quality change.* London: Department of Health.

Department of Health (2005b). *Coronary Heart Disease National Service Framework: Leading the way. Progress report.* London: Department of Health.

Department of Health (2005c). *Chief Executive's Report to the NHS: December 2005. Statistical supplement.* London: Department of Health.

Department of Health (2005d). *Government Response to the Health Committee Report on the Influence of the Pharmaceutical Industry.* Cm 6655. London: The Stationery Office.

Department of Health (2004a). *The NHS Cancer Plan and the New NHS: Providing a patient-centred service.* London: Department of Health.

Department of Health (2004b). *The NHS Improvement Plan: Putting people at the heart of public services.* London: The Stationery Office.

Department of Health (2004c). *Choosing Health? Making healthier choices easier.* London: Department of Health.

Department of Health (2004). *Winning the War on Heart Disease: Progress report.* London: Department of Health.

Department of Health (2003). *The NHS Cancer Plan: Three year progress report.* London: Department of Health.

Department of Health (2001). *The Expert Patient: A new approach to chronic disease management for the 21st century.* London: Department of Health.

Department of Health (2000a). *The NHS Plan: A plan for investment, a plan for reform.* London: The Stationery Office.

Department of Health (2000b). *The NHS Cancer Plan.* London: Department of Health.

Department of Health (2000c). *Coronary Heart Disease: National service framework for coronary heart disease – modern standards and service models.* London: Department of Health.

Department of Health (1999). *National Service Framework for Mental Health: Modern standards and service models.* London: Department of Health.

Devlin N, Parkin D (2004). 'Does NICE have a cost effectiveness threshold and what other factors influence its decisions? A binary choice analysis'. *Health Economics,* vol 13 (5), pp 437–52.

Dixon J, Lewis R, Rosen R, Finlayson B, Gray D (2004). *Managing Chronic Disease: What can we learn from the US experience.* London: King's Fund.

Dixon T, Shaw M, Frankel S, Ebrahim S (2004). 'Hospital admissions, age and death: retrospective cohort study'. *British Medical Journal,* vol 328, pp 1288–90.

Feachem RGA, Sekrhi NK, White KL (2002). 'Getting more for their dollar: a comparison of the NHS with California's Kaiser Permanente'. *British Medical Journal,* vol 324, pp 135–43.

Filmer D, Pritchett L (1999). 'The impact of public spending on health: does money matter?'. *Social Science and Medicine,* vol 49, pp 1309–23.

Fireman B, Bartlett J, Selby J (2004). 'Can disease management reduce health care costs by improving quality?'. *Health Affairs,* vol 23 (6), pp 63–75.

Fisher ES, Welch HG (1999). 'Could more health care lead to worse health?'. *Hospital Practice,* 15 November, pp 15–26.

Fisher ES, Welch HG (1999). 'Avoiding the unintended consequences of growth in medical care: how might more be worse?'. *Journal of the American Medical Association,* vol 281 (5), pp 446–53.

Fogel RW (2004). *The Escape from Hunger and Premature Death, 1700–2100: Europe, America and the Third World.* Cambridge: Cambridge University Press.

Freemantle N, Hill S (2002). 'Medicalisation, limits to medicine, or never enough money to go around?'. *British Medical Journal,* vol 324, pp 864–65.

Garnier JP (2005). 'A prescription for combating global diseases'. *Financial Times,* 30 May, p 15.

Gravelle H, Blackhouse M (1987). 'International cross-section analysis of the determination of mortality'. *Social Science and Medicine,* vol 25, pp 427–41.

Hall RE, Jones CI (2004). *The Value of Life and the Rise in Health Spending.* National Bureau of Economic Research Working Paper 10737. Cambridge, MA: National Bureau of Economic Research.

Ham C (1999). 'The role of doctors, patients and managers in priority setting decisions: lessons from the "Child B" case'. *Health Expectations,* vol 2 (1), pp 61–69.

Hanson MJ, Callahan D (1999). *The Goals of Medicine.* Washington, DC: Georgetown University Press.

Harrison A (2003). *Getting the Right Medicines?* London: King's Fund.

Harrison A (2002). *Public Interest, Private Decisions*. London: King's Fund.

Harrison A, Appleby J (2005). *The War on Waiting for Hospital Treatment*. London: King's Fund.

Harrison A, New B (2000). *Access to Elective Care*. London: King's Fund.

Healthcare Commission (2004). *State of Healthcare Report*. London: Healthcare Commission.

Health Service Journal (2005). 'Reid warning for service: record funding is set to end'. *Health Service Journal*, 21 April, p 5.

Hertz E, Hebert JR, Landon J (1994). 'Social and environmental factors and life expectancy, infant mortality and maternal mortality rates: results of a cross-national comparison'. *Social Science and Medicine*, vol 39, pp 105–14.

House of Commons Health Committee (2005). *The Influence of the Pharmaceutical Industry*. London: The Stationery Office.

Institute of Medicine (2001). *Crossing the Quality Chasm: A new health system for the 21st century*. Washington, DC: National Academy Press.

Institute of Medicine (2000). *To Err is Human: Building a safer health system*. Washington, DC: National Academy Press.

Jack A, Bowe C (2005). 'Shock treatment: drugs companies seek new remedies to restore growth'. *Financial Times*, 21 April, p 17.

Jenkins DJ, Kendall CW, Marchie A, Faulkner DA, Wong JM, Emam A, Parker TL, Vidgen E, Laspley KG, Trautwein EA, Josse R, Connelly PW (2003). 'Effects of a dietary portfolio of cholesterol lowering foods vs lovastatin on serum lipids and C-reactive protein'. *Journal of the American Medical Association*, vol 290 (4), pp 502–10.

Jones CI (2002). *Why Have Health Expenditures as a Share of GDP Risen So Much?* National Bureau of Economic Research Working Paper 9325. Cambridge, MA: National Bureau of Economic Research.

Kasper JF, Mulley AG, Wennberg JE (1992). 'Developing shared decision-making programs to improve the quality of health care'. *Quality Review Bulletin*, vol 18 (6), pp 183–90.

Kendrick S (1996). 'The pattern of increase in emergency admissions in Scotland'. *Health Bulletin*, vol 54 (2), pp 169–83.

King's Fund (2005). *An Independent Audit of the NHS under Labour (1997–2005)*. London: King's Fund.

Kwangkee K, Moody PM (1992). 'More resources better health? A cross-national perspective'. *Social Science and Medicine*, vol 34, pp 837–42.

Le Fanu J (1999). *The Rise and Fall of Modern Medicine.* London: Little Brown.

Le Grand J, Mays N, Mulligan J eds (1998). *Learning from the NHS Internal Market: A review of the evidence.* London: King's Fund.

Leatherman S, Sutherand K (2003). *The Quest for Quality in the NHS: A mid-term evaluation of the ten-year quality agenda.* London: The Stationery Office.

Lichtenberg F (2003). 'Pharmaceutical innovation, mortality reduction and economic growth' in *Measuring the Gains from Medical Research: An economic approach,* Murphy KM and Topel RH eds. Chicago: University of Chicago Press.

Lichtenberg F (2002). *Benefits and Costs of Newer Drugs: An update.* National Bureau of Economic Research Working Paper 8996. Cambridge, MA: National Bureau of Economic Research.

Lichtenberg F (2001). *The Benefits and Costs of Newer Drugs: Evidence from the 1996 medical expenditure panel survey.* National Bureau of Economic Research Working Paper 8147. Cambridge, MA: National Bureau of Economic Research.

Mackenbach JP (1996). 'The contribution of medical care to mortality decline: McKeown revisited'. *Journal of Clinical Epidemiology*, vol 49 (11), pp 1207–13.

Mango PD, Riefberg VE (2005). 'Health savings accounts: making patients better consumers'. *McKinsey Quarterly*, January.

Maynard A, Boor K, Freemantle N (2004). 'Challenges for the National Institute for Clinical Excellence'. *British Medical Journal*, vol 329, pp 227–29.

McGlynn E (1998) *Assessing the Appropriateness of Care: How much is too much?* Santa Monica, CA: RAND Research Briefs.

McGlynn EA, Asch SM, Adams J, Keesey J, Hicks J, DeCristofaro A, Kerr EA (2003). 'The quality of health care delivered to American adults'. *New England Journal of Medicine*, vol 348, pp 2635–45.

McKee M (1999). 'For debate: does health care save lives?'. *Croatian Medical Journal*, vol 40 (2), pp 123–28.

McKeown T (1979). *The Role of Medicine: Dream, mirage or nemesis?* Oxford: Blackwell.

Melzer D, Zimmern R (2002). 'Genetics and medicalisation'. *British Medical Journal*, vol 324, pp 863–64.

Miller RD, Frech HE (2000). 'Is there a link between pharmaceutical consumption and improved health in OECD countries?'. *Pharmacoeconomics,* vol 18, supp 1, pp 33–45.

Mintzes B (2002). 'Direct to consumer advertising is medicalising normal human experience'. *British Medical Journal*, vol 324, pp 908–09.

Moldrup C (2005). 'No cure, no pay'. *British Medical Journal*, vol 330, pp 1262–64.

Moynihan R, Heath I, Henry D (2002). 'Selling sickness: the pharmaceutical industry and disease mongering'. *British Medical Journal*, vol 324, pp 886–91.

Munro J, Sampson F, Nicholl J (2005). 'The impact of NHS Direct on the demand for out-of-hours primary and emergency care'. *British Journal of General Practice*, vol 55 (519), pp 790–92.

Murphy KM, Topel RH eds (2003). *Measuring the Gains from Medical Research: An economic approach*. Chicago: University of Chicago Press.

National Audit Office (2005). *Emergency Care*. London: The Stationery Office.

National Audit Office (2004). *Tackling Cancer in England: Saving more lives*. Report by the Comptroller and Auditor General, HC 364 Session 2003–2004. London: The Stationery Office.

National Audit Office (2002). *NHS Direct in England*. Report by the Comptroller and Auditor General, HC 505 Session 2001–2002. London: The Stationery Office.

NHS Modernisation Agency (2004). *10 High Impact Changes for Service Improvement and Delivery*. London: Department of Health.

Neumann PJ, Sandberg EA, Bell CM, Stone PW, Chapman RH (2000). 'Are pharmaceuticals cost-effective? A review of the evidence', *Health Affairs*, vol 19 (2), pp 92–109.

Newhouse JP (1992). 'Medical care costs: how much welfare loss?'. *Journal of Economic Perspectives*, vol 6 (3), pp 3–21.

Newhouse JP (1977). 'Medical care expenditures: a cross-national survey'. *Journal of Human Resources*, vol 12 (1), pp 115–25.

Nolte E, McKee M (2004). *Does Healthcare Save Lives? Avoidable mortality revisited*. London: The Nuffield Trust.

Nordhaus WD (2003). 'The health of nations: the contribution of improved health to living standards', in *Measuring the Gains from Medical Research: An economic approach*, Murphy KM and Topel RH eds. Chicago: University of Chicago Press.

Or Z (2001). *Exploring the Effects of Health Care on Mortality Across OECD Countries*. Labour Market and Social Policy Occasional Papers No. 46, Paris: Organisation for Economic Co-operation and Development.

Organisation for Economic Co-operation and Development (2004a). *Economic Survey: United Kingdom, 2004*. Paris: OECD.

Organisation for Economic Co-operation and Development (2004b). *Towards High-performing Health Systems*. Paris: OECD.

Organisation for Economic Co-operation and Development (2001). *OECD Health Data 2001*. Paris: OECD.

Pauly M (2003). 'Should we be worried about high real medical spending growth in the United States?'. *Health Affairs*, January web exclusive, pp W3–15.

Picker Institute (2005). *Is the NHS Getting Better or Worse?* Oxford: Picker Institute.

Pirmohamed M, James S, Meakin S, Green C, Scott AK, Walley TJ, Farrar K, Park BK, Breckenridge AM (2004). 'Adverse drug reactions as cause of admission to hospital: prospective analysis of 18,820 patients'. *British Medical Journal,* vol 329, pp 15–19.

Pritchard A (2004). 'Measuring government health services output in the UK national accounts: the new methodology and further analysis'. *Economic Trends*, vol 613, December, pp 68–81.

Propper C (2001). *Expenditure on Health Care in the UK: A review of the issues.* Centre for Market and Public Organisation Working Paper. Bristol: Centre for Market and Public Organisation, University of Bristol.

Propper C (1990). 'Contingent valuation of time spent on NHS waiting lists'. *The Economic Journal*, vol 100, pp 193–99.

Ryan M, McIntosh E, Dean T, Old P (2000). 'Trade-offs between location and waiting times in the provision of health care: the case of elective surgery on the Isle of Wight'. *Journal of Public Health Medicine*, vol 22, pp 202–10.

Scottish Executive (2005). *Funding for cancer drug development*. Press release, 8 February.

Secretary of State for Health (2005). *Creating a Patient-led NHS: Work in progress*. Speech to the New Health Network, 7 November.

Segal L, Day N, Day S, Dunt D, Piterman H, Robertson I, Hawthorne G (2003). *Evaluation of the Southern Health Care Network Coordinated Care Trial*. Melbourne: Centre for Health Program Evaluation.

Seshamani M, Gray A (2004a). 'Ageing and health-care expenditure: the red herring argument revisited'. *Health Economics,* vol 13, pp 303–14.

Seshamani M, Gray A (2004b). 'A longitudinal study of the effects of age and time to death on hospital costs'. *Journal of Health Economics*, vol 23, pp 217–35.

Sikora K (2002). 'The impact of future ethnology on cancer care'. *Clinical Medicine,* vol 2 (6), pp 560–68.

Smith SD, Heffler SK, Freeland MS (2000). *The Impact of Technological Change on Health Care Cost Increases: An evaluation of the literature*. Working paper. Baltimore, MD: Health Care Financing Administration.

Stearns SC, Norton EC (2004). 'Time to include time to death? The future of health care expenditure predictions'. *Health Economics*, vol 13, pp 315–27.

Strategic Policy Making Team (1999). *Professional Policy Making for the Twenty-First Century*. London: Cabinet Office.

Szreter S (2000). 'The McKeown thesis'. *Journal of Health Services Research and Policy*, vol 5 (2), pp 119–21.

Taylor D (2003). 'Fewer new drugs from the pharmaceutical industry'. *British Medical Journal*, vol 326, pp 408–09.

Technical Review Panel on the Medicare Trustees Reports (2000). *Review of Assumptions and Methods of the Medicare Trustees' Financial Projections*. (Accessed 24/8/04: www.cms.hhs.gov/publications/technicalpanelreport/)

Wang L (2002). *Health Outcomes in Low-Income Countries and Policy Implications: Empirical findings from demographic and health surveys*. Working paper No. 2831. Washington, DC: World Bank.

Wanless D (2002). *Securing Our Future Health: Taking a long-term view. Final report*. London: HM Treasury.

Wanless D (2004). *Securing Good Health for the Whole Population. Final report*. London: HM Treasury.

Wennberg JE (2004). 'Perspective: practice variations and health care reform – connecting the dots'. *Health Affairs*, web exclusive, October 7.

Wennberg J (1987). 'Are hospital services rationed in New Haven or over-utilised in Boston'. *Lancet*, vol 8543, pp 1185–89.

Wolfe BL (1986). 'Health status and medical expenditures: is there a link?'. *Social Science and Medicine*, vol 22, pp 993–99.

Wolman M, Manor R (2004). *Doctors' Errors and Mistakes of Medicine: Must health care deteriorate?* Amsterdam: IOS Press.

World Bank (2005). *Improving the World Bank's Effectiveness: What does evaluation show?* Washington DC: The Independent Evaluation Group, World Bank.

World Health Organisation (2000). *The World Health Report 2000 Health Systems: Improving performance*. Geneva: WHO.

Zahl P-R, Strand BH, Maehlen J (2004). 'Incidence of breast cancer in Norway and Sweden during introduction of nationwide screening: prospective cohort study'. *British Medical Journal*, vol 328, pp 321–24.

Zweifel P, Felder S, Meiers M (1999). 'Ageing of population and health care expenditure: a red herring?' *Health Economics,* vol 4, pp 485–96.

Zweifel P, Manning WG (2000). 'Moral hazard and consumer incentives in health care' in *Handbook of Health Economics,* Culyer AJ and Newhouse JP eds, vol 1, part 1, pp 409–59. Amsterdam: Elsevier.

How Should we Deal with Hospital Failure?
Facing the challenges of the new NHS market
Keith Palmer

One in four NHS trusts in England ended 2004 in deficit. The impact of current NHS reforms will be to magnify financial imbalances at a significant number of trusts, with the risk that some of them will fail. But there is no real plan for dealing with failure in the NHS. This paper outlines proposals for dealing with financial instability by heading off failure before it happens and introducing a regime to manage those failures that cannot be averted. It emphasises the need for mechanisms that not only restore financial viability, but also protect the quality of patient care.

December 2005 ISBN 1 85717 542 5 60 pages £5.00

The War on Waiting for Hospital Treatment
What has Labour achieved and what challenges remain?
John Appleby, Tony Harrison

The need to wait for hospital treatment has been a feature of the NHS since it began. When Labour came to power in 1997, total numbers waiting stood at 1.3 million, and the government announced a 'war on waiting'. This paper begins with a description of the task the government faced and assesses the policy initiatives it has taken to address it. It also looks at what the government should do next. The paper draws on previous studies by the King's Fund into waiting list policy and the ways in which individual trusts have responded to national targets.

August 2005 ISBN 1 85717 496 8 96 pages £15.00

An Independent Audit of the NHS under Labour (1997–2005)
King's Fund

The Labour Party came to power in 1997 promising to 'save' the NHS. Since then it has invested unprecedented levels of funding in the health service, but has emphasised that the extra money must be linked to 'reform'. This audit, commissioned by *The Sunday Times*, assesses the Labour government's performance against its targets to bring down waiting times; recruit more health care professionals; and improve care in cancer, heart disease and mental health.

March 2005 ISBN 1 85717 488 7 88 pages £20.00

How Much Should We Spend on the NHS?
Issues and challenges arising from the Wanless review of future health care spending
John Appleby, Nancy Devlin, Diane Dawson

The 2002 Wanless report on NHS spending, *Securing Our Future Health: Taking a long-term view*, had a significant impact on the future of health care in the United Kingdom, informing spending plans for the NHS, and leading to unprecedented increases in public spending. But it also laid out a framework for revisiting the fundamental question: how much do we want to spend on health care? To set out its costed 'vision' of the NHS in 2022, the report made assumptions, such as the likely impact of changing demographics on health care spending. Drawing on a one-day seminar convened by the King's Fund, the Office of Health Economics and the Centre for Health Economics at the University of York, this publication explores the assumptions, estimates and models underlying the spending recommendations of the Wanless report.

July 2004 ISBN 1 89904 087 0 146 pages £12.50

What is the Real Cost of More Patient Choice?
John Appleby, Anthony Harrison, Nancy Devlin

At first glance, an increase in patient choice seems to be unequivocally 'a good thing'. But what trade-offs are really involved – and what price are we prepared to pay? And how far can individual freedoms be extended while retaining the essential objectives of the NHS? This discussion paper sets out the questions that the government needs to answer if it wants to place patient choice at the heart of a health care system funded by tax-payers. These include how extra costs will be met, whether patients are willing and able to exercise choice in their own best interests, and what kinds of limits to choice might be needed.

June 2003 ISBN 1 85717 473 9 64 pages £6.50

Hidden Assets
Values and decision-making in the NHS
Bill New, Julia Neuberger

A modern, publicly owned health service inevitably has to balance competing priorities, such as equity of access and increased patient choice, or efficiency and effectiveness. This publication – based on a series of King's Fund seminars with senior policy commentators, managers and academics from both sides of the Atlantic – examines what values and ethics really mean for the NHS, and asks how staff and policy-makers can resolve these issues. Combining analysis with case studies, it shows how values can successfully translate into health care provision, and argues that if values are to 'live' as an organisational reality, trade-offs must be visible, managed and explicit.

March 2002 ISBN 1 85717 458 5 230 pages £17.00

Contested Decisions
Priority setting in the NHS
Chris Ham, Shirley McIver

Every day, NHS managers face difficult choices about funding patient care. Decisions about whether to fund expensive drugs or treatment can be fraught with difficulty for everyone concerned. This publication uses five real-life case studies to draw out the implications of these difficult decisions for patients, doctors and managers. It argues that conflicting interests are inevitable at times, and suggests ways in which doctors and managers can handle these. By using good communication, involving independent experts and drawing on peer support, doctors and managers can help everyone involved feel that the situation has been satisfactorily resolved. The publication is a sequel to *Tragic Choices in Health Care: The case of child B.*

September 2000 ISBN 1 85717 418 6 154 pages £10.99

Tragic Choices in Health Care
The case of child B
Chris Ham, Susan Pickard

The case of Jaymee Bowen, known as 'Child B' during the court case surrounding her future, has come to epitomise the dilemmas involved in making tragic choices in health care. When Jaymee needed life-saving cancer treatment for the third time, she was refused funding, despite a court appeal by her father. This publication examines the implications of difficult decisions of this nature for patients, doctors, managers and others, and makes recommendations for how cases of this kind should be handled in the future
May 1998   ISBN 1 85717 203 5   100 pages   £10.99